Introduction to Tac Hacking:

A Guide for Law Enforcement

Jeff Neithercutt

POLICE TECHNICAL
Technical. Training. Solutions.

Terre Haute, Indiana

4

POLICE PUBLISHING dba POLICE TECHNICAL

661 Poplar Street, Terre Haute, IN 47807, USA

Copyright © 2015 POLICE TECHNICAL. All rights reserved.

No part of this book may be reproduced in any form, electronic or mechanical, including information storage and retrieval systems, without written permission from the Publisher. Reviewers may quote brief passages.

This publication and its individual parts are protected under copyright by the Publisher.

Designed by POLICE PUBLISHING dba POLICE TECHNICAL.

Manufactured in the United States of America

Brand names listed in this publication are protected by their trademarks.

Library of Congress Cataloging-in-Publication Data

Neithercutt, Jeff

Introduction to Tactical Hacking: A Guide for Law Enforcement

ISBN: 978-1-63180-008-5

Paperback

Copies of this book are manufactured using Print on Demand.

Contents

Author's Note 7

Introduction 8

Prologue: Tactical Hacking in Action 9

    How could Tactical Hacking have helped? 10

    Preparing to gather intelligence for your target 11

Chapter 1: Fourth Amendment Issues 14

    How to start a discussion with the DA: 15

    How to explain it to your Supervisors: 16

    How to explain it to the Jury: 17

    How to document it in your report: 20

Chapter 2: Networks 21

    The basics 21

Chapter 3: Hardware and Devices 29

    Computers: 29

Chapter 4: Building a Tactical Hacking Lab 33

    Faraday Bags 35

    Enumeration 36

Chapter 5: Tactical Hacking Field Platforms 38

    Kali Linux Installation Procedure: 39

    To Begin Installation: 39

Chapter 6: Building a Tactical Hacking Tablet 46

Chapter 7: Tactical Hacking Wi-Fi Scanner 60

Chapter 8: Reconnaissance Tools 65

Chapter 9: Collecting Cellular Data 75

Chapter 10: The Best Policies, Procedures and Practices 86

Acknowledgements 97

Glossary 98

    About POLICE TECHNICAL 107

    Police Technical National Courses 2016 107

    In-Service Training 108

    Additional POLICE TECHNICAL Books 109

Author's Note

I will endeavor in this book to provide you with an overview of free or low cost ways you can build a Tactical Hacking platform for you and your department to use to save people's lives. I will start with the basics about all things computers, then move into chapters specific to each of the types of technology I think you will need to be well versed in.

Please get your local District Attorney, City Attorney, and any necessary three letter agencies in your area on board before using any of these devices and abilities, but I am here to tell you, based on my training and experience, you can do these things, and if done right, you can use them to save lives.

The public has made it clear that they no longer trust Law Enforcement in many arenas, and the use of this type of technology will, at times, be compared to "Big Brother." It will be critical that you answer the public's concerns about your use of this type of technology so that they don't form incorrect assumptions about its use.

Once you begin to deploy any of the tools/tactics described in this book, engage some type of community forum where people can ask the obvious questions about when and where you will be authorized to use it, whether you will need a warrant, and whether the use of this technology will be tracked/monitored/reported on by anyone other than your agency.

In the interest of simplicity, I've used the word "Target" throughout this book to apply to the subject of your investigation. This will be a "Hostage Taker" in some scenarios, and a "Barricaded Subject" in others, but either way, the word Target is used to draw your attention to the fact that the subject being discussed is who/what is the subject of your investigation.

Ensure you have a policy in place allowing your use of the tools/equipment you have in your lab, in the field, and at home, so that when spurious accusations begin flying, you can disprove them quickly. I also highly recommend you achieve the Certified Ethical Hacker certification available at http://www.eccouncil.org/Certification/exam-information/ceh-exam-312-50, or any other professional certifications that will allow you legitimacy in this field.

I achieved a National University's Master's Degree in Cyber Security and Information Assurance with a specialization in Penetration Testing and Ethical Hacking, and I highly recommend that course, available here:

http://www.nu.edu/OurPrograms/SchoolOfEngineeringAndTechnology/ComputerScienceAndInformationSystems/Programs/Master-of-Science-in-Cyber-Security-and-Information-Assuranc.html.

Introduction

When it comes to the latest technology, Police are woefully behind, and efforts to catch up have been severely hampered by budgetary constraints, regulatory restrictions, and lack of training. As a result, officers, SWAT Operators, and Police Personnel at all levels of service are not making full use of the available technologies that could provide critical, life-saving intelligence.

Additionally, the Corrections component of Law Enforcement has been struggling for some time to deter unauthorized cellular phone use in their facilities by the inmates. I think that is an admirable quest, but I would also encourage them to consider how the peer-to-peer chat functions within the Wi-Fi capabilities of a Smartphone could be used to run prisons on the inside, allowing inmates to have entire communications networks between themselves without ever even activating the cellular functions of the phone.

This book is designed to introduce Law Enforcement personnel at all levels to technology available right now. Simply defined, Tactical Hacking is development and redesign of existing tools, software, and technology to access, intercept, interrupt, or utilize a suspected source of information technology to save lives. How is it being used by those around us, how is it being used against us, and how we can better use it to assist our efforts to do our jobs?

It is not intended to be used in an everyday investigation, but, rather, when a subject is armed, threatening others, and/or is barricaded in a building. The information I present in this book isn't even secret. Civilian Penetration Testers have been using these tools, in some cases, 10 years or more. Still, Law Enforcement remains very unfamiliar with the technology or its life-saving potential uses.

What I will attempt to do here is make the technology available in a way that talks specifically about our unique perspectives, needs, tactical considerations, and mission critical functions so that Law Enforcement can protect themselves and those they serve from those who would harm or exploit us.

Remember: get permission, in writing, and always consult with your Supervisors and District/State and Attorneys General before activating any of the strategies I suggest in this book. Also, understand that you will always need a warrant at some time during the process of using this type of intelligence gathering equipment and tools. So when you get the situation stabilized, and there is time to request it, get a warrant completed and in front of a Judicial Authority as soon as possible. You have the right to use these tools, but that right hinges on authority that will wane with the passage of time without a signed Court Order to support it. It might also be a good idea to draft a policy concerning its use, as well.

Jeff Neithercutt
August 2015

Prologue: Tactical Hacking in Action

I'll begin with a description of an actual event that occurred in Sacramento in June, 2010. The incident involved Anthony Alvarez, a 25-year-old murder suspect also wanted for robbing three banks in the San Francisco Bay Area and shooting at a Concord Police Officer during a traffic enforcement stop the day prior [See Figure 1]. Alvarez was holed up in an apartment complex using his adult cousin's family as hostages during a 56-hour-long multi-jurisdictional SWAT standoff. It ultimately ended with his death and the rescue of one-year-old Michael Pittman, who was unhurt other than an abrasion on his leg.

Alvarez had successfully delayed SWAT Operators entry into the apartment by sporadically spraying gunfire and using the one-year-old as a shield.

Figure 1: Anthony Alvarez, a 25-year-old murder suspect involved in a deadly standoff

According to a debriefing I attended in 2014, one of the biggest challenges the Hostage Negotiations Team [HNT] faced when trying to peacefully recover Alvarez's hostages was that he would hang up his cellular phone, then use it to call his relatives. This prevented HNT from reestablishing contact with Alvarez, sometimes for many hours. As the HNT member who gave the debriefing expressed his many frustrations from this incident, three struck me as valuable to the subject of Tactical Hacking.

Alvarez controlled his cellular phone and the HNT Operators suffered long waits and frustrating disconnections because they had to rely on the cellular provider to give interrupts on Alvarez's cell phone. Then, all they could do was dial back and hope Alvarez would answer.

Because the SWAT operation lasted 56 hours, multiple SWAT teams with varied technological abilities and equipment became involved. It was common for an established communication line with the suspect to be torn down and re-established by the relieving SWAT team because their technologies were not interchangeable.

The debriefer sincerely believed he could have successfully convinced Alvarez to surrender peacefully if HNT could control Alvarez's cellular phone and communications with the outside world. I am not here to armchair quarterback that event. It ended the way it ended, and I am confident the SWAT and HNT Operators did the best they could with the equipment, manpower, and training they had at their disposal.

That said, Alvarez never made any demands and his mother described him as "not in his right mind," so it is highly unlikely additional abilities to communicate with him would have changed the outcome, but it certainly might have made the SWAT and HNT operator's jobs easier and safer to perform. His use of his phone could have been more strictly controlled by removing the customer service reps at Metro from the loop.

HNT might have allowed Alvarez to make the calls he wanted, but then disconnected them to use the minutes Alvarez needed to speak with family as bargaining chips. HNT could have listened in on the calls Alvarez was making to hear whether he was telling people he was scared and wanted to surrender, or was making plans to set booby-traps and take as many officers with him as he

Introduction to Tactical Hacking: A Guide for Law Enforcement

could. Either scenarios would have drastically changed the direction the SWAT teams were taking in negotiations with him.

Ideally, when a barricaded suspect is engaged, Tactical Hacking provides SWAT Team Leaders with information about the suspects exact location, what tools he may have, whether he is monitoring TV news stations, accessing his Facebook, posting on Twitter, emailing, texting, making calls, and what the content is of all of those outside contacts. This is all so the suspect's frame of mind can be monitored.

Knowing that your barricaded suspect just posted on Facebook that he is scared and wants to surrender but can't figure out how to reach SWAT members is a critical piece of information to a successful and peaceful resolution.

Knowing that your barricaded suspect is searching Google and YouTube with subjects like, "Homemade bombs," "DIY Booby-Traps," "Homemade Anti-Personnel devices," and "IED's for Dummies" can also provide the needed intelligence for Operators to act before the suspect becomes more heavily barricaded or constructs said devices.

How could Tactical Hacking have helped?

A Tactical Hacking Operator would have approached Alvarez's barricaded position with an eye on access and sustained control over his communication resources. An overview of the building and interviews with other occupants would determine the type of lines occupants used for telephone, television, Internet, or any other electronic gadgetry installed – for instance, the newer Home Automation Control systems for heating and air, alarm controls, and security camera systems.

After seeing their options, I'm certain the SWAT and HNT Operators utilized each of those devices, as well as others they brought with them, like throw phones, a short range walkie-talkie, or anything else they could come up with to establish communications.

Once they figured out Alvarez had Metro PCS as his cellular provider, SWAT and HNT initiated the appropriate exigency protocols to establish wiretap and interrupt/intercept permissions on Alvarez's phone. It all sounds good so far, but what happens when the process to get Metro to interrupt Alvarez's phone calls to his relatives takes 15 minutes, and then he doesn't answer the phone when HNT calls?

Cellular phone providers have dealt with an assortment of issues related to installing infrastructure throughout their service areas over the explosive 20-year cellular phone system build out. Most of their customer complaints have likely centered on coverage, particularly in outlying areas where it is either too expensive or geographically infeasible to install a tower.

As a result, cellular providers developed mini cellular towers that use the customers' own high-speed Internet connection to establish an Internet connection to the cellular provider's network, then broadcasts a cellular signal from the mini cellular tower. This makes customers think they have "five bars digital service" from a local outdoor cellular tower.

These mini cellular towers have many technical names: Femtocell, Microcell, "Air Raid," and other proprietary names assigned by the providers. Metro PCS offers the same type of device and, once installed and operational, Metro engineers can instruct on-scene officers/operators on how to drive the suspect's cellular device off the existing Metro tower nearby and force association with the Tactical Cellular device controlled by the SWAT or HNT personnel.

By the way, you should definitely build a relationship with a 24/7/365 employee you can reach at every cellular phone company with service in your jurisdiction, if you can arrange it. Nothing beats a well-trained human with connections, in my experience.

One of the other frustrations the HNT debriefer expressed was that Alvarez had moved himself to a position within the home out of sight of the SWAT operators and officers. This greatly increased their concern for the safety of one-year-old Michael, as they could not determine if he was being properly cared for, or was potentially being used as a human shield by Alvarez.

Many of today's modern entertainment centers provide possible solutions to those outside who wish to legally monitor the activities of those inside. For instance, there has been much hype in the media about "Smart TV's" being programmed to detect whether there is anyone actually in front of them, so that advertisers can be assured their commercials are actually viewed. It is possible to access these devices remotely and either take over control of their functions to exploit the audio or video technology built into them for legal surveillance purposes. Most importantly, you can pipe a video feed directly to the TV from a command post nearby with a family member pleading with them to give up, which might cause them to move into sight, or remain in a specific room.

Additional communication points:
- XBOX gaming console Kinect
- Video baby monitor/ audio baby monitor
- VOIP phone systems with a speaker phone
- Printers with a phone connection for Faxing
- DVRs such as Tivo, Dish Network, and DirecTV boxes
- Wireless/wired networks on a laptop, home computer, tablet, or phone

Preparing to gather intelligence for your target

It is important to follow six steps every time:

1. Intelligence Gathering:

Intelligence Gathering requires access to social media, Law Enforcement, publicly available databases, as well as outside resources like local friends, relatives, neighbors, and work associates. Even animals the target holds dear can be helpful in a negotiation with a barricaded suspect. You need to gather as much information about your target as possible, using any means necessary, and recording who/what the resource is, so that if needed later, you can use the intel in the future. Remember, you may be back to this address many times, or you may encounter this individual at another time elsewhere.

2. Threat Modeling:

Finding the assets most likely to provide you with access to your Target involves enumerating [scanning] for available networks he has used or generated. All wireless Internet services are broadcast over the air, which means with an antenna, you can monitor, manipulate, or compromise pretty much anything within reach. Cellular, Bluetooth, and Wi-Fi scanners can help determine which assets you would be most successful in attacking. It is critical to know what your Targets skillset is, and you need to be aware of possible counter-surveillance techniques he might deploy against you. Remember, when you open a connection to the Target network, it's open both ways. Any hole you open you need to be constantly monitoring so that it doesn't end up becoming a liability for you. We'll talk later about sandbagging and sandboxing your network tools to prevent them from giving anything away about you, while still being capable of gathering intelligence about your Target.

Introduction to Tactical Hacking: A Guide for Law Enforcement

3. Vulnerability Analysis:

Spend as much time as you need locating flaws in the Target's computer systems and applications so that you can leverage multiple vectors of attack at the same time. You may find a minor flaw in his firewall that will only annoy him, but while distracting him with that, he may miss you slipping through a backdoor on his router to plant permanent solutions to your surveillance needs. This is why we will talk about lab versus field tool deployment options. You don't rush a barricaded shooter armed with a long rifle with just your handgun and body armor when you have a rifle and armor plates in your car. You also should try to bring every tool with you when you go, as each situation will change rapidly and just one tool seriously hampers your ability to switch up your tactics if your Target throws a curve at you, or detects, or even disables one of your tools. Part of VA will involve social media investigations and exploitation as well, so bone up on that when you get the chance. POLICE TECHNICAL just released a book by Jennifer Golbeck called *Introduction to Social Media Investigation* and it is an excellent primer on utilizing social media to gather information about your target.

4. Exploitation:

Once you establish the vector of attack you will use, and the vulnerabilities you will try to exploit, focus on gaining access to a specific system most likely to deliver the information you need. You will bypass security restrictions in this phase, if you locate any. Most home computer network systems are poorly configured for security, if they are configured for security at all. However, working in the SF Bay Area near Silicon Valley, I know for a fact there are people in my jurisdiction with better computer security skills than me, so try to be stealthy here. Being detected while breaking into someone's computer system may cause more harm than you think. If you are successful and gain administrative access on one system, preserve that access and maintain it. You may be able to use it to escalate privileges on a trusted machine somewhere else on the network that will provide you with even more leveraged access than the original machine. But once you close the door behind you, it may be difficult, or impossible, to re-open. Also be aware that your target may become paranoid, angry, or offended if they detect you bit fiddling their network, and it could trigger nastiness toward your hostages, so work with your Incident Commander to determine whether to conduct your exploitation "low and slow" or "quick and dirty." You want your IC to know at all times if you gain access, and also if you believe you've been detected or compromised. It could drastically affect the hostage negotiation process, or it could dramatically improve it. Either way, your IC needs to know what you know and be in the loop as to your progress. You also need to be planning your next moves 5 steps ahead so that your documentation efforts are easier and more succinct. If you are taking video or still shots/screen shots as you move along, your after action report will go much smoother, and you may find it easier to remember which tool you used, and in which order.

5. Post Exploitation:

After you gain access to a machine and have secured that access by creating a second administrative account or opening another way in, try to evaluate what you've gained with this machine, and see if it has any other information about nearby resources, other networks in the area you hadn't been aware of, or additional resources connected to the machine that weren't immediately obvious to you. Install additional accounts or access devices on each machine to guarantee that even if the Target reboots or disconnects your access for a few minutes, you'll be able to reestablish access at a later time.

6. Reporting:

You should carefully document and record everything you do to gain, maintain, and manipulate access to each device on the Target network. You will need to be able to articulate exactly how you gained access, what you used to gain access, and what you did while you had access to each and every network resource you compromise during your Tactical Hacking expedition. Additionally, you should be able to reproduce the attack completely in a test lab for later demonstration, and you should be able to document what you gathered of an evidentiary nature for the Search Warrant Return that somebody, if not you, will eventually have to complete and get back to the Judge.

Chapter 1: Fourth Amendment Issues

Your department, like mine, operates on a healthy diet of policies and procedures that are usually very well defined, or deliberately vague, depending on who wrote them and what they are designed to do. Prepare a document for your policy manual that defines the following items for all Tactical Hacking engagement activities, so you aren't left trying to explain something to a Command Staff member on-site, mid-crisis.

A solid document defines the general scope and latitude your department will allow for most, if not all, Tactical Hacking engagements. The scope should be prepared with input from your Command Staff, and be reviewed frequently. This document should be referred to throughout your report when you are discussing the systems you attacked and the techniques you used. For Instance, "I used the [tool] against [target ID] as defined in the [agency] scope document for approximately X minutes and learned the following…"

Goals:

Brainstorm with your Tactical Commanders on what your goals should be when first responding to a Tactical Hacking incident. Generic goals are "Gather Intel on available networks" and "locate Internet service provider information and demarcation point." A demarcation point is the place on the side of most houses or businesses where the cable or phone lines enter the building. It is an important location for determining the type of Internet and network the house/business is wired for, and also an easy place to access for tapping or MITM devices. Targets can also be a pre-defined area where the operations plan is just a fill-in-the-blank for the name, but the actual location and type of assessments could be pre-filled.

Techniques:

Specify, in advance, the tools you're using to your Command Staff, and the SWAT team, so they will know the types of intel you can provide and how you will access it. Being up front about not being willing to use certain tools and techniques is also critical; tell your Command Staff that you will not use any tool you aren't comfortable with. This is common in our field. The K9 handler decides when to send in the dog. The SWAT commander decides when to force entry and move, and the Tactical Hacker has to be ready and willing to say, "No denial of service attacks" if he is unable to verify leakage that might harm outside networks, or if launching one might compromise the TH's position and stance.

Reasonable Expectations:

Work with your teams and Command Staff to make them aware of what you and your tools capabilities. Give them a realistic timeframe for tools like brute force password attacks that could take minutes, hours, days, or even weeks to accomplish. It is my opinion, and, I believe, backed up also by legal precedent, that once you have established the legal right to use lethal force to stop a target's actions, you are generally allowed to use any other level of force, including search and seizure without a warrant in exigent circumstances, to gather whatever information or resources you can from the target in order to attempt to peacefully resolve the situation.

That said, get the District Attorney, or whomever occupies that position in your particular local legal system, on board with your plan first. You need to verify that they understand what you are proposing to use in the way of tools and access, and that they agree with you that it is legal, or at least an acceptable risk to use these tools and procedures, when you are gathering information that you might not otherwise be able to gather without judicial authorization, either in the form of a search or arrest warrant, or some other judicial process.

Attempt to gain understanding from them of the time period after the exigency arises after which they will no longer accept exigency in place of a warrant. This will give you a target time period within which to request one.

In the earlier example of the Arden Way standoff in Sacramento, you would be hard pressed to argue that there was no time during that 56 hours for someone in your organization to write and request authorization of a warrant for your activities.

How to start a discussion with the DA:

Case Law surrounding Exigencies:

In Ker V. California, 374 U.S. 23 (1963) the United States Supreme Court ruled that Police can enter a residence without a warrant to prevent the imminent destruction of evidence. If you can articulate that your target is possibly either in the process of destroying, or is about to destroy evidence of a crime you are actively investigating, you are allowed to enter the residence without a warrant.

Granted this is a California case. However, it was a US Supreme Court ruling, so it covers the entire jurisdictional area they are responsible for. If your target is within the United States, or an outlying area the Supreme Court has jurisdiction over, this ruling should apply. However, you should verify with your local judicial authority that you are covered by this particular ruling so that if your target is conducting activity you can articulate reasonably led you to believe he was destroying evidence, you should be legally allowed to interrupt that activity in an effort to preserve that evidence.

Ask your judicial authority:

- Whether he would allow, authorize, or accept you using an interception or interference tool to prevent, deter, or stop detected activity that led you to believe your target was trying to delete files on their computer systems.
- Whether he would allow, authorize, or accept you taking action to intercept, interfere, or deter activity you can articulate could render digital evidence inaccessible, such as the suspect actively encrypting their hard disks, or particular files on their hard disk.
- Whether he would allow, authorize, or accept you accessing your target's digital devices and changing their password to lock them out of the device if you detected attempts to destroy, encrypt, or otherwise render the device inaccessible if you had reason to believe there was digital evidence on their device.
- Whether he would allow, authorize, or accept remotely copying or dumping the data on your target's digital devices to an area for storage and eventual processing for evidentiary value.
- Whether he would allow, authorize, or accept your setting up a "spoofed" wireless Internet device that could fool devices in your target's control into connecting to them because of a previously established trusted relationship between those devices and the name or indicator of the trusted device.
- Whether he would allow, authorize, or accept evidence you collected while conducting a "MITM" [Man in the Middle] attack against your target for the purpose of monitoring, intercepting, controlling, and manipulating voice, data, picture, or textual information sent or received by your target.
- Whether he would allow that same MITM access on the target's cellular usage, i.e., setting up a "spoofed" cellular connection, "fake" cellular tower, or the use of the commercial devices like the "Stingray."

Introduction to Tactical Hacking: A Guide for Law Enforcement

How to explain it to your Supervisors:

Supervisors are an interesting breed. They come from a vast range of educational backgrounds and work histories. This presents a real challenge when attempting to explain this type of technology, but it can and should be done before you utilize any of the procedures described herein. They may be very suspicious of the technology and just outright dismiss it. Provide a small, lightly technical demonstration of the capabilities you are testing out, or even a YouTube video will open the dialogue.

Even if it doesn't work, and you can't get the supervisor on board, don't give up. Approach your tactical operators instead. Also stress the patrol side of Tactical Hacking, and the permissions we have to use this technology that also won't require a warrant. Here's an example:

Victim calls Dispatch and reports that while showering at the local health club, his cell phone "disappeared" from the bench in the changing room. He is pretty sure it was stolen, but isn't really interested in charging anyone, he just wants the phone back. You meet the victim on a residential street surrounded by apartments and he tells you he has a cell phone tracking application [FindMyIphone] on his other phone and it is "pinging" his missing cellular phone "right there" and he points to a detached garage surrounded by parking lot.

You have two options at this point. You can take a report, request a search warrant for the garage [denied, not enough evidence indicating the item is inside, or that the person who has it did so maliciously], and proceed with a criminal investigation. However, this will take up valuable patrol resources for hours working a phone theft case that, at least in California, will end up being a misdemeanor [as long as the phone is valued under $950.00].

Or, you can identify your victim's home or work Wi-Fi network SSID [Starbucks], activate your cellular phone's "hotspot" technology, and change your hotspot's name to match. Then, wander around the area broadcasting that SSID until you see your victim's phone connect and authenticate (*victimphoneMACdd:00:87:83:12:HY). At that point, you can not only corroborate your victim's statement that the phone is in the area, but also verify that the phone is within a much smaller area than with the FindMyIphone application, which is using GPS and cellular triangulation.

You can later testify that the device has to be within 30 to 300 feet because that is the limit for a cellular device without amplification using Wi-Fi. You could then start up your Kali laptop and run Netstumbler, or some other network signal tracking tool, and key in the MAC address [remember *victimphoneMACdd:00:87:83:12:HY]. Then, use your directional antenna to attenuate signal strength as you approach the device until you are so close you could reach through the wall and touch it. Finally, knock on the door, ask for the device back, and drive away with a happy victim. There's no report to write, and only 30 minutes spent [or less after you get better at it].

This argument will get your supervisor very interested, particularly as more and more people come to Police looking for "Civil Standby" type services while they "retrieve" their "lost" items from potentially scary characters.

There are many variations on how this technology can potentially save hours of patrol time, but the really valuable demonstration of this is after a supervisor witnesses it work a few times, you mention how valuable that device tracking ability could be for a wanted suspect, or kidnapped victim, or a device taken in a violent crime like an Armed Robbery or a Carjacking. This device tracking ability could gain you definitive evidence that a suspect in a specific apartment or house is your target.

How to explain it to the Jury:

Civilians are frequently unaware that a target may be well known to the department or recently involved in some sort of violent confrontation, particularly if they are taking hostages or making threats to injure or harm themselves or other people. Explaining to a jury law enforcement's views on people who have either weapons or the threat of weapons can be difficult.

For most people, as they say, "ignorance is bliss." In this situation, begin with a brief description of your background in technology, covering how you became familiar with it as well as the target you used it on. Also explain how and why you deployed the technology, so the jury has a better understanding of exactly what you were facing.

For instance, in the following scenario, a 911 call comes into your local dispatch center from a concerned family member who states that an adult male member of the household with a history of mental health issues has recently had his medication changed. Since he began taking new medication, his behavior has grown increasingly hostile.

The arriving officers contact the target inside the front porch area of the home and the officers describe the target as being paranoid, confrontational, and not complying with commands to show his hands or put down something that he may be carrying.

When asked to accompany the officers to a vehicle in the front yard for additional discussion, the suspect refuses and retreats into the house, threatening to kill anyone who tries to follow him.

As officers begin to gather intel about the target, dispatch advises that the original 911 call came from a family member inside the residence who identified herself as the target's mother and explained that she was bedridden and afraid of the target. The mother was asking for police to respond to evaluate the target for potential mental health commitment on a 72-hour hold, as well as assistance and advice in moving to an assisted living care facility for herself, where the unreliable and increasingly confrontational behavior of the target is no longer a concern to them.

Based on the threat of violence to anyone who follows the target into the residence the officers retreat to a position of cover, set up a perimeter and call for support in the form of additional perimeter units, and request additional resources stage nearby, including fire and ambulance.

Officers attempt to call back into the residence on the line that was used for 911 to call out and they make contact with the target who states that his mother is "fine" and refuses to allow the officers to speak to her. The target further states that anyone who comes into the house will be shot.

A routine records check of the target indicates that he has purchased several handguns in the past and contact with other family members indicates that he also has access to long guns inside the residence.

The SWAT commander is contacted and a SWAT call out is initiated and the technical officer is sent to the scene with a Kali laptop and advised to begin enumeration attempts in an effort to discover any additional resources that could be used to gather either surveillance or intelligence information.

The information requested includes where the target is inside the residence, who else may also be inside the residence with him, and whether he is using the Internet, cell phone, or other technology to speak with anyone inside or outside of the home.

The technical officer starts up the Kali laptop and uses a Wi-Fi scanner in the form of NetStumbler and Wireshark to determine that there is a wireless router and an HP printer broadcasting an SSID from within the house.

The technical officer is also able to ascertain that there is a femtocell inside the residence that is a sprint based cellular device, and by using a cellular scanner [like HackRF One] locates two cellular signals that appear to be originating from within the residence.

Introduction to Tactical Hacking: A Guide for Law Enforcement

The SWAT team arrives and begins deploying resources around the building and tosses a throw phone through the window in an attempt to establish and maintain communications with the target, who is no longer answering the landline.

Eventually the suspect surrenders and the information gathered by the technical officer and the SWAT team members are then entered into a report. If you were the Technical Officer in this situation, how would you explain the initial approach to the building and your efforts to ascertain the types of signals emanating from the residence? How would you describe what electronic resources the signals you detected most likely indicated were in use inside the residence, and what tools you used to determine that?

How would you describe these items in a fashion that a member of the jury with little to no computer skills would be able to understand?

With a rough sketch of a house and just some simple hash marks around the outside edges that you can explain to the jury are radio waves that you are able to pick up with an antenna, you might be able to describe basically to the jury what you did.

But an actual demonstration of NetStumbler with a cell phone device in Wi-Fi mode across the courtroom might be better, so that the jury can literally see what you saw when you first picked up the target's cell signal. Describe how you used a directional antenna and software attenuator to verify that the signals you were picking up were actually emanating from inside the house, not the house next to or behind the target.

Using directional antennas like a Yagi or similar style antenna, you could provide a simple signal finding and attenuating [turning the signal down until you can't pick it up unless you are right on top of it] demonstration that could be very powerful to a Jury.

This could be critical to your case in a more crowded environment like an apartment building or condominium complex, as it would be much more difficult not only to determine which signal belongs to the target, but also to be able to show a jury later how you were able to differentiate between the target's Wi-Fi signal and that of his next door neighbor.

It could be critical to be able to say for certain in a court of law that the signal you were monitoring belonged to the target, particularly if they were eventually charged, beyond a reasonable doubt.

Also, should force be used to that causes someone to be greatly injured, or lose their life, your testimony could be a pivotal point in both a criminal and the eventual civil trial. This type of demonstration would be a good way to show how you were able to pick up the signal, particularly if done in a way that a jury would be able to follow.

It will become critical in most criminal, and some civil trials, to be able to explain to the jury why you couldn't just sit back and wait, rather than continuing to try to reach out to the target. It may require you explaining why negotiations with the target deteriorated to a level where the decision was made to force entry and rescue the hostage rather than continuing to attempt negotiations with the target.

You need to understand and be aware of the fact that someone from a generation who grew up without computers, or without the technology that you will be describing, and that you used in this tactical incident, may not understand what you are saying. Your ability to explain complex technology and concepts can be critical to your testimony being well received, understood, and even agreed with by members of the jury.

You need to make sure that the demonstrations you give are age and experience appropriate for the members of a jury, members of the press, members of your command staff, and even members of the general public wherever possible. Sometimes people who don't understand the technology may dismiss the credibility of the person who uses the technology out of fear, or lack of understanding about the technology.

Keeping your demonstration simple, drawing basic diagrams, presenting your diagrams and evidence to the DA or members of the public who may be friends of yours and not particularly

Chapter 1: Fourth Amendment Issues

technically savvy themselves, can help you to verify that regular citizens can follow what you're saying, and that it makes sense. This is an excellent way to test your presentation before you get in front of the jury, to make certain that it's going to be understandable, and not too technically complicated, or "deep in the woods" for the individuals who will be exposed to it.

The general public may understand what you're saying about the technical tools and purpose of your tactical hacking, but understanding why you were doing that, and what legal authority you had to do that, may be even more important than understanding what you did. The district attorney or your judicial authority should assist you by laying that foundation for you before you even get to the stand. But make sure that when you meet with the judicial authority, before going to court and testifying about what you did, they understand what your legal authority was and what your intentions were in using the tools that you used.

Make sure they understand what the information was that you gathered with the tools that you used, and how the information was preserved once you gathered it, and where the evidence was stored.

Review information that you got that was of evidentiary value, and make sure you understand how it was stored prior to being admitted into evidence in the case. Verify that you used, documented, and completely understood the Chain of Custody you kept with the devices, tools, hardware, software, and digital evidence.

It will not be "enough" to say, "After monitoring the cell phone communications of the subject and recording the communications with my digital audio recorder, I uploaded the digital audio into our digital evidence server." Any Defense Attorney is going to quiz you on how you "know" that the evidence you collected is the same as the evidence you are presenting in court.

Your ability to testify that you used a "hashing" tool to digitally compare the evidence when you collected it, and when you reviewed it later in court, and the "hashing" tool revealed the same digital signature on both, and what exactly that means will be critical.

It will be critical to the defense to try to poke holes in your tools, qualifications, and education. Keeping in mind that members of the jury are frequently members of the community who are retired, unemployed, medically unable to work, or for some other reason able to serve on a jury for an extended time without working, be aware of the fact that someone from a generation that grew up without computers and without the technology that you will be testifying that you used will be critical. It's also going to be critical that your testimony is received, understood, and even agreed with by members of the jury.

If the defense is able to successfully squash that testimony, the case is likely to be dropped or overturned on appeal, and rightfully so, that is the "reasonable doubt" premise upon which our legal system relies.

If you are testifying that your target said, "I'm going to kill you" in a text message to your victim, you have to be able to say with confidence that it was your target that said that in the text message, and that your target was the person that sent the text message, and that it was the target's phone that generated the text message, and that you are confident the threat was intended for the victim.

It's much easier to do that with a handwritten note than it is with a series of electronic signals snatched out of the air with an antenna from a location remote to your target. If the defense attorney can successfully convince the jury that either your tactics, your tools, your equipment or your integrity is unreliable, then all the evidence you collected will be tainted by that reasonable doubt, and you're likely to lose that case.

If you are able to convey to the jury that your purpose in turning on your tactical hacking equipment and using your tactical hacking software was to protect the officers responding to the incident as first responders, establish reliable and consistent communications with the target, and with the goal first and foremost of ending the tactical incident peacefully, you are much more likely to have them accept the evidence that you collected.

Introduction to Tactical Hacking: A Guide for Law Enforcement

If they thought you were using tactical hacking specifically to try and gather evidence necessary merely for prosecution, particularly if the individual on trial has any sort of mental health issues or other compelling reason for the jury to feel sorry for them, you will have a difficult time winning their support.

How to document it in your report:

Documentation of who what when why and where is probably far less critical in a tactical hacking situation than the how. It makes no difference if you are able to write a report that talks about who what when why and where if the person reading the report doesn't understand how you gathered that information.

We've heard it said a thousand times, "if it isn't in your report it didn't happen." This is particularly true with tactical hacking because you're asking people to believe that you stuck a wire up into the air and magically gathered information from a suspect a hundred yards away from you that incriminates him, or that provided you with the impetus to force entry into his residence to rescue someone because you felt their safety was threatened.

Anyone reading a police report needs to be able to understand exactly what led you to the conclusion that the level of force you later used was justified. You can put conclusions and opinions on your report all day long, but without backing those opinions and conclusions up with solid, articulable facts, they are just that, opinions and conclusions.

What makes something evidence is using documented, established, policies, procedures and tools to identify, collect, and analyze it, then show how it directly or circumstantially links your target to the crime being investigated.

Just as it is critical in a drunk driving case to be able to describe in clear accurate terms exactly what it was about the way the subject performed the field sobriety tests that led you to the opinion that they were under the influence, and then to the conclusion that they were impaired to a level that they were either a danger to themselves, or others, and should not be operating a motor vehicle; it will be critical in a tactical hacking case to be able to describe in your report, using clear, concise descriptions of the technology you used, the signals that you discovered, and how you associated those signals with the suspect.

In order for you to form the opinion that they were emanated by the target, and eventually led you to the conclusion that they were of evidentiary value, and threatening in nature either to the officers responding, or the subjects being held against their will inside the target location, you will have to establish how the signals you collected establish that.

Your ability to clearly articulate how the devices you use function, what their purpose is, and how you were able to determine with the information gathered from those tools that the suspect in your investigation was the person who generated the evidence you collected, will be a critical part of your report.

You should make certain that you thoroughly understand, at least to the level of being able to basically describe, sketch, or teach someone who doesn't understand anything about the technology you used, to a basic user level of understanding, before you attempt to testify about any data that you may have collected.

The bottom line is, don't use tools that you don't understand, and make certain whatever you collect comes from your target, and that you can prove it.

Chapter 2: Networks

The Basics:

Simply stated, a network is "a group or system of interconnected people or things."[1] A network can be devices, as with computer networks, or it can be a "sneaker net," which is a group of people who share information by walking back and forth and passing notes to each other or talking. Let's talk a little about the construction and configuration of a computer network, particularly where it comes to assigning addresses to devices within the network.

A network is basically just a series of devices that all use a common technology that they can share information over. This technology can be based on electricity and frequently has a delimiting function to it that allows you to discern more accurately what type of information is being sent and to what type of device.

With networks, devices can more accurately record, access, store, and retrieve data from local, remote, and distant locations. Networks occur in nature, as in the case of the Kentucky Mammoth Cave system, and the root structure of Mangrove Trees, which apparently allow them to communicate in some fashion, though I'm not really sure what they have to discuss.

In the case of computers, a network is created to allow a computer system to access devices that it would not otherwise be able to access. For instance, rather than buy each computer in your office a cheap bubblejet black and white computer, why not buy one expensive color LaserJet printer with a network port, connect it to the network, and give every computer on the network access to it.

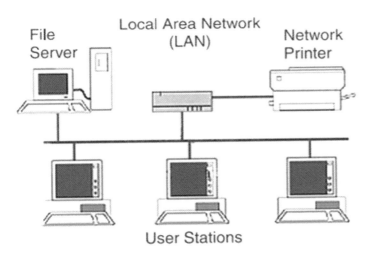

Figure 2: Workstations are connected by wire/wireless router to a File Server and a Network Printer.

In the basic network diagram [See Figure 2], several workstations, or single user computers, like the one in your report writing area or on your desk at work, are connected by wire, or wireless router, to a File Server and a Network Printer:

This allows each workstation access to the services and functions that a file server can host, like internal web pages, Computer Aided Dispatch and Records Management software, even a centrally located hosted Faxing network.

It also makes it possible to provide a basic computer workstation with the capability to do color scanning, faxing, copying, and file storage of large video and audio files in a centrally located system that can be backed up regularly to an off-site location for security and redundancy.

So how does the workstation know about the server, and the server and workstation know about the printer?

Addressing. That is the short answer. The long answer is that a network is just basically like your neighborhood at home. Think of your neighborhood as a network, with 40 houses, one fire

---

[1] https://www.google.com/webhp?sourceid=chrome-instant&ion=1&espv=2&ie=UTF-8#q=definition%20of%20network

Introduction to Tactical Hacking: A Guide for Law Enforcement

station, one police station, one post office, and one hospital. Each business in the neighborhood would be the web sites that end in .com [commercial], while each church, police department, and hospital can have an address ending in .org [organization].

Each home has an address inside your neighborhood with numbers and a street name. Fire station, police departments, post offices, and hospitals all provide services to every house in the neighborhood, so they would be like a network fax server, file server, printer, or tape backup system.

The post office provides mail services to the neighborhood, and is the only one that knows for sure who mails what from inside the neighborhood to outside the neighborhood, and provides delivery of return mail back to the house from outside the neighborhood, as well. It is the Post Office's responsibility to keep track of each resident at the house, and to make sure that what you order or request by mail gets delivered from you to the vendor in the outside world, and that your order, when returned by the outside vendor, gets delivered to you, at your house.

The Police Station, Fire Station, and Hospital all know about your home address, and sometimes are aware of the name of each resident inside, but not always, and certainly not as up to date as the Post Office does.

The Police Station, Fire Station, and Hospital all wait for you to request services from them, where the Post Office will actually bring you things you requested, and keep track of your requests into and out of the neighborhood.

Using this analogy, the streets in your neighborhood become the network lines [wired or wireless] depending on your technology, and vehicles could be the data packets that carry the information requested to and from the addresses in your neighborhood. You direct the vehicle you own, and your neighbor directs his vehicle to and from the addresses he wishes to go, just as you direct the data coming in and out of your computer to the websites you request information from.

If someone were to break into your vehicle, he could see your information, so think of data encryption as driving an armored vehicle [Bearcat] instead of a car. The data could still be captured, but it would take a LONG time to break into because of the armor surrounding it.

So, the rest of the world has neighborhoods too, and their systems work the same way. You can send and receive data to and from them via cars on the roads just as your computer sends and receives data to and from the world over network cables.

In order to keep track of all of the neighborhoods, they created an addressing system that could scale [grow and shrink] to meet the number of resources inside each neighborhood, as it grew, shrank, changed, etc.

This addressing system is called subnetting, and the mathematical explanation makes my brain hurt, so let me just explain. Each country has the first three digits in the address, each city has the next three, each neighborhood has the next three, and each house has the last three.

So if your address was 123 Main Street, Sacramento, United States, the address would be written like this:

USA.SAC.MAN.123, or in computer language, depending on the carrier, 102.152.251.123, where 102 is the assigned code for USA, 152 is the assigned code for Sacramento, 251 is the assigned code for Main Street, and 123 is the house number.

The Post Office in each neighborhood is most like the DNS servers used throughout the Internet to translate URL [Uniform Resource Locator] from www.yahoo.com, which is non-routable [can't be sent or received to or from because the address is invalid] to its actual numerically assigned designation of 206.190.36.45, which is routable [can be sent to and from by networked devices].

Since the Post Office [DNS Server] maintains regularly updated address lists, it learns from all of the other Post Offices [DNS Servers] where each and every web site, or business, is physically housed based on its assigned physical address, and uses routing tables to keep the lists, which it then shares with every other Post Office frequently so that the addresses of every business and computer can be updated accurately.

Each community is assigned a Class A, Class B, or Class C address, and that designates how many addresses the community can have. Because each address can be subnetted by splitting the numbers mathematically, a Class A starting with the nation number example from earlier USA.xxx.xxx.xxx can have a total of 2,147,483,648 assigned device addresses within it, a Class B starts with the nation and city so USA.SAC.xxx.xxx and can have a total of 1,073,741,824 addresses in it, and finally the Class C address starts with USA.SAC.MAN.xxx and can have a total of 536,870,912 addresses.

Obviously, I am greatly simplifying a very complicated mathematical process, but you get the gist of it, and really, you don't need to understand the math side of this process unless you are designing, implementing, or installing networks. Also, you need to understand that anything that starts with 192.xxx.xxx.xxx is non-routable on the outside network. If you assign your lab network non-routable addresses, then it will be impossible for your lab computers to be seen, or to see neighborhoods outside the lab.

Understand, however, also that if you point a gun at a target, you can shoot it, even if you aren't supposed to, so make sure before you fire off some of the tools I discuss in this book, you are certain of your target, and that you have limited your shot to exactly that target only. Don't rely on subnet limiting routability to protect your tools from hitting, or even damaging, or attacking other networks in range. Many Hacker tools are designed specifically to not follow the rules related to how networks are supposed to work based on ICANN standards. Think of them as a hand grenade. If you throw a hand grenade at your target, it will hit your target, but will also shrapnel anything else in range.

Also understand that this example is only based on the existing IPV4 Internet addressing standard, soon to be replaced with IPV6, which works very similarly, but has infinitely more devices available because it uses 8 fields with four alphanumeric fields EACH, which provides it the ability to assign a total of 2 to the 128th power devices addresses within an IPV6 network. That is so huge, I don't even want to waste the paper to print it out.

Thinking of IPV6 using the same example I've given above, and again, super simplified compared to the mathematical portion, with IPV6 you will have the ability to do this:

My toaster, installed in my kitchen, at 123 Main Street, City of Sacramento, State of California, USA, North America, Earth, or EART.NOAM.USA1.CALI.SACT.MAIN.0123.KITC.TOAS, which would make it possible for my toaster to send and receive information across the Internet, because it could be addressed properly end to end with all other routable Internet addresses.

This makes a lot of Internet communication available to things it was not available to with IPV4 addressing, hence this new term being bandied about, "The Internet of Things." Your toaster can send you a text when your toast is done, and you can tell it to re-toast the bread in it to warm it up. Your refrigerator can detect when you are down to the last eight ounces of milk, and notify your milk vendor to send it some more.

Your dog food container can text you when Fido's bowl is low and your dog food container can order another bag of Kibbles and Bits from Amazon when it detects you are a week away from Fatso going hungry.

This is a quantum leap in computer addressing technology, making a lot of things much easier, and a lot of things more complicated. For instance, errands such as going to the grocery store will not be necessary anymore, as your refrigerator will notify Amazon that you need cheese A drone will be dispatched to deliver it, your home routing system will receive, process, and deliver the cheese to the refrigerator, and your card will be charged, all without you needing to lift a finger beyond setting up the payment process ahead of time.

Introduction to Tactical Hacking: A Guide for Law Enforcement

However, it will become infinitely more difficult to detect where bad guys are hiding, as they can spoof (clone) addresses belonging to devices too simple to know they should report they've lost network connectivity, and your search for a subject who purchased a bunch of things on your victim's credit card will dead end when you discover the source of the crime was a ceiling fan in Nigeria.

Every request you make on a computer gets packaged into little things called data packets. Each data packet contains a header, the data, and a destination address. The shape and design of a data packet is very similar to a bullet, so let's use that as an analogy.

So a bullet, like a data packet, is made up of multiple parts. The bullet itself is usually a thick metal piece, sometimes jacketed with a thin layer, sometimes not.

If you think of a jacketed round as a dense center chunk with a thin metal jacket around it, this is very similar to what is knows in network parlance as "encapsulated data," or "encrypted data." A data packet that needs to be sent across the network without someone being able to read it if captured in the middle of the transmission is sort of like a bullet being stopped in mid-flight where the manufacturer has put a thick or impenetrable cover over it, so that even if the bullet is captured mid-flight, you will never be able to see what is in the middle.

Encrypted packets work in exactly the same way, only the bullet (data you don't want to be read or understood), is mathematically scrambled by a piece of software, then wrapped in a coating of digital armor, before being fired down the network cable. You can picture firing a bullet in the air and realize that even if they wanted to, a bad guy interested in capturing that particular bullet fired from that particular gun would have a practically impossible task figuring out how to be in the right place at the right time to intercept a randomly fired round like that.

Once fired, the bullet (data packet) travels a specific path depending on where it's aimed. Unlike a bullet, however, a data packet is addressed to a specific location depending on it's function. Like a bullet, this path does usually follow a straight line, similar to a barrel, however, once it has reached the target, it can continue on to another target.

It can also "hang a right" or redirect itself if a router/switch or other network device in the path determines the path is blocked, or a better path exists than that already being travelled. Think of it as a "homing bullet", where the bullet knows where it's target is, and will take whatever path necessary to get to the target, no matter how long or convoluted the path, or how far the distance to reach it.

Go back to the addressing description I gave earlier, and pretend we are giving that bullet (data packet) the 123 Main Street address. We fire it from the keyboard via the application layer by using an application to create and address it. Huh?

Picture yourself sitting in front of the computer. You open your email application (Outlook, web browser [gmail, yahoo, hotmail, AOL] and you write an email to your boss at 456 Main Street in New York, USA. The email application is in the application layer of the 7 layer OSI model. You can find that at http://www.escotal.com/osilayer.html.

The email is assembled and properly encapsulated in data packets properly addressed for your boss, then the email is passed to the Transport layer, where, based on the type of data it is [email.eml] it is scheduled for transport via TCP [Terminal Control Protocol] and because your computer is attached to the Internet via network cable [or Wi-Fi] it is passed to the Network Layer and converted to IP standards [Internet Protocol]. The easiest way to think of this is as a translation layer.

All types of computers using all types of operating systems and all types of computer language are all connected to the Internet. Rather than having every computer contain every operating system with every possible computer language, which would require us all to have incredibly expensive and large computers, standards committees form protocols and standards that all computers can use to be able to send things to each other that they will understand.

24

These types of translation standards are generally assigned to specific transportation technologies like the Internet, email, FTP [File Transfer Protocol], HTML [Hyper Text Markup Language] which is what the world wide web (Internet) uses to properly format and display web pages for every type of computer on the planet with a web browser, which is an application designed to read HTML.

After the email is converted to the proper format for transmission across the Internet, it is passed to the Data Link Layer, where it's address is examined by the local sending service (think post office) and passed down the closest link to the next post office, and the next, until it reaches it's destination, where it is converted by the New York post office back to Internet Protocol, delivered by the Transport Layer which converts it back to it's original format [email.eml] and delivers it to the application at the destination server.

Networks use this "packet-switching network" topology [way of routing signals] to most effectively route the trillions upon trillions of packets of data that pass over the Internet daily. If one area of the Internet becomes congested due to heavy traffic, then the routers around it sense this delay [known as network latency] in processing their signal requests, and re-route their data by other nearby routers that are less congested.

Understanding the order that the system boots in can assist you in not only troubleshooting your own computer issues, but also in figuring out where to "shim the stack."

"Shimming the Stack" is a computer term used to describe using hardware or software to insert some type of a tool into the computer processes in order to observe, interrupt, alter, corrupt, or sabotage your target system. The "stack" is more frequently a description used to relate to the series of steps each data packet travels when leaving and returning to a computer. Each layer in the "stack" relates to a particular piece of hardware or software within the computer, and most can be "shimmed" in more than one way.

The TCP/IP Stack (Terminal Control Protocol/Internet Protocol) is the most common Stack you will encounter with the tools and processes described in this book, so let's talk about that for a minute. Try to stay awake, this stuff can get pretty deep in the weeds, but it's important for you to understand because you may find yourself having to explain it on the stand someday, if you're lucky.

Every data packet sent by any application on your computer passes through this same process, as does every data packet received by your computer. The data packet travels back UP through the same stack on the receiving computer, or yours, if it is just returning from the web.

Going back to the bullet analogy I used to describe a data packet above, the MAC address [Media Access Control] is physically assigned to every network connected piece of hardware you have. Think of it as a physical address you could write a letter to, sort of like the address in the Toaster analogy above. The only problem is, it's not quite that secure or consistent.

In fact, only the application layer ever even needs to know or interpret your MAC address, because it is assigned only to your network card, on your computer [and every other computer built exactly the same way as yours if you bought a mass produced one like a Dell or HP], the rest of the information needed to transmit your data from your laptop to it's destination is handled by the IP address. Remember that USA.SAC.MAN.123 address? That series of numbers 192.168.152.123 tells the computers and routers between your system and your boss's system where your data packet needs to go.

Once it arrives, the application receiving it from the network card it was addressed to, will see and add the MAC address to it, but it really isn't necessary for external traffic. Internally though, the MAC address tells the system which device requested the information so that the system can keep track of system requests for data processing and make sure information is routed efficiently, and according to the assigned priority.

Some of the data is unique, some is not, and some may be "spoofable," which is to say that a person may be able to use hardware or software to pretend to be someone else. In this case, it

Introduction to Tactical Hacking: A Guide for Law Enforcement

would be like someone creating a new house, somewhere in another part of the world, but giving it your home address, and making every post office in the world think their copy of your house is actually your house.

When you are thinking about a network and data travelling across it, think of any video you've ever seen of a military grade machine gun firing at night in the desert somewhere. There are "tracer" rounds going out that you can see, and depending on the gun, ammunition, and purpose, they are fired every X number of bullets.

So, for instance, if the machine gun is capable of 3,000 rounds per minute, the tracer round might be mixed in every 10 rounds or so, which means you would see a round mixed in with the regular bullets every 50 rounds or so, and it would look weird, because your eyes are telling you there are far fewer rounds flying through the air than the sound of the machine gun is telling your ears it is firing.

Data packets are very similar in nature and you could think of your suspect computer as the machine gun, and each bullet it is firing out is a data "packet." Just like a bullet, a data packet is made up of many parts, except that a data packet may actually have more, or fewer parts, every time it is fired, depending on the purpose, sort of like a tracer round.

The tracer round is designed to do one thing, show the person firing the weapon, in a brilliant visible way, where the bullets are flying, so that the person firing can have feedback on his shot placement, and verify it is roughly matching the sight picture and intended destination of the rounds.

Bullets are like data packets, except that most data "packets" [bullets in this analogy] contain many different interchangeable parts, depending on the purpose, destination, and whether a return receipt or "ack" [short for acknowledgement] is required.

Imagine you have a paper target 50 yards downrange, and you are firing an M4 [automatic firing AR15 platform rifle] at the target, but every fifth round that leaves the barrel not only is brightly visible [tracer] while flying through the air, but once it impacts the target, it sends up a flag saying "made it!!" or other messages like, "got it, send more" or "got it but it was broken send again" or "got it but you aren't authorized to shoot at me, so I'm returning it unopened." This is how network data travels across the network, arrives at its destination, and queries the sender for more.

A bullet, like a data packet, is made up of multiple parts. The bullet itself is usually a thick metal piece, sometimes jacketed with a thin layer, sometimes not. If you think of a jacketed round as a dense center chunk with a thin metal jacket around it, this is very similar to what is knows in network parlance as "encapsulated data," or "encrypted data."

A data packet that needs to be sent across the network without someone being able to read it if captured in the middle of the transmission is sort of like a bullet being stopped in mid-flight where the manufacturer has put a thick or impenetrable cover over it, so that even if the bullet is captured mid-flight, you will never be able to see what is in the middle.

Even if you encrypt your data, an awful lot of information in the "Header" (tip) of the data packet remains unencrypted so that the routers (Post Offices) along the path it is taking can see where it came from, and more importantly, where it needs to go. This unencrypted data can be used to determine a lot about the data inside the encrypted packet, so it is best to try and anonymize the data in the Tip as much as possible.

Onion, or "TOR" networks accomplish this by spreading out your data packets over a bunch of random participating Post Offices on the internet so that no single Post Office knows all of the information related to where the data came from, or is heading to, so "Traffic Analysis" techniques can't be used (as easily) to establish things like size, destination, timing of travel, or source, in an effort to determine what is hidden in the encrypted traffic.

This technique is basically Data Counter Surveillance. Just as when you want to make sure you aren't being followed home from the station, data packets in the TOR network hide in various different locations, turning and twisting through hundreds of Post Offices, and trying to take a random path from the source to the destination. This prevents a single observer in any one portion of the trip from seeing both the true source and true destination of the data. As the data passes through each routing point along the way, only the last data point and the destination data point is seen by the current routing partner, so no single capture of the data can reveal it's true source or destination unless it is captured at the last TOR router, known as the "exit node", and even that point can only see which router the data last passed through, not the originating router.

This process is how Tor works. It makes it infinitely harder to track data because the header with travel instructions is unencrypted and re-encrypted as it passes through each router and hardware piece in the stack and between machines. Obviously, the more devices and routers the packet passes through, the more secure and difficult tracking and decrypting the packet will become.

Encrypted packets work in exactly the same way, only the bullet [data you don't want to be read or understood], is mathematically scrambled by a piece of software, then wrapped in a coating of digital armor, before being fired down the network cable.

However, because the Internet requires connections via wired or wireless networks, a hacker has a much less difficult time figuring out where to be to intercept communications from or to a specific location/person/device.

There are literally billions of different connections across the Internet [See Figure 3], but they are on predictable, even mappable paths called links.[2] Each link or leg

Figure 3: Illustrated above is a 2015 map of the entire Internet conducted by a group called the "Opte Project."

has a number assigned to it that is called an "IP Address." Think of this address as almost the same as the address on a house. If you send mail to a house it gets delivered to the address. If you send data to a specific device or computer, it is delivered to the IP Address assigned to that particular device or computer.

You can deduce the IP Address of a specific device or computer in many ways, but the easiest is to send a data packet to a known individual and "sniff" the network traffic leaving from, or arriving to, a specific device or computer. Basically, you can stand out in front of the house and wait for the mailperson, read the mail, then deliver it to the mailbox at the house. This is a simplified explanation of a "MITM" or "Man in the Middle" attack. You intercept data bound for a specific address, read it, then deliver it, and if you are careful, the destination computer or device is never aware you did so. They receive the data they were expecting and are none the wiser that it was intercepted in transit.

We can manipulate this process to Tactically Hack a subject who has barricaded himself and/or taken hostages, in order to determine his state of mind, plans, and to force or control his communications capability in order to resolve the situation peacefully.

---

[2] Image provided by http://www.opte.org/.

Introduction to Tactical Hacking: A Guide for Law Enforcement

Here, we are focusing our attention on their specific Internet or network connected devices, in the location where they are now, by capturing data streams they are sending or receiving from any data capable device, over any medium, whether wired or wireless. Think of it like a perimeter being set up around their house. No one gets in or out without our authorization, scrutiny, and monitoring.

If the target subject is inside the target area, we need to put up electronic fences that will act like a bullet sponge, catching, or at least detecting, any bullets [data] being sent or received by the target.

Chapter 3: Hardware and Devices

Computers:

A car has many parts, as does a computer. Ironically, they work very similarly. The car has a frame and body; the computer has a case. The car has a windshield; the computer has a screen. The car has a gas tank, the computer has a hard drive. The car has a fuel line; the computer has RAM [random access memory]. The car has a steering wheel; the computer has a mouse. The car has a battery; the computer has a power supply. The car has a carburetor; the computer has a CPU [central processing unit].

Inside the case is a power supply. This is a lot like a battery in a car, except that it requires constant power in the form of an electric cord plugged into the wall to provide electricity, which the PSU (power supply unit) converts to current that the computer needs to operate:

The PSU provides power to the motherboard, which is very much like the engine in a vehicle. The motherboard receives electrical signals from the various parts of the computer, like the keyboard, mouse, and other input devices like Hard Drives, USB drives, CD Rom and DVD drives, and it re-routes those signals to the areas they need to be manipulated, first via RAM, then to the screen for viewing.

All incoming signals pass through the IO bus [Input/Output] into RAM, which is the only place the data can be changed. In our car analogy, the request for data flows from the outside air into the intake manifold through the carburetor, where the data requested meets it from the gas tank [hard drive] through the fuel line [RAM]. The larger the fuel line and carburetor, the faster the flow of fuel and air, the faster the engine can run, so if you upgrade your RAM you are just installing a fatter fuel line, and if you upgrade your hard drive you are just installing a larger tank to hold the gas. When you replace your CPU you are going from a two barrel carb to a four barrel carb.

Introduction to Tactical Hacking: A Guide for Law Enforcement

Looking at this motherboard below, the long yellow and blue strips at the bottom are the RAM ports, or fuel line. The more chips inserted in these slots, the larger the fuel line, the faster the system.

The white box is where the carburetor goes, so when you upgrade your CPU to a faster chip, you are going from a two barrel carb to a four barrel carb. Black or gold finny looking things are heat sinks to prevent the chips on your motherboard from overheating, very similar to the radiator fins on the radiator in your vehicle keeping the coolant cool as it circulates through the engine to keep it from overheating and seizing up.

A CPU is just like a carburetor. It takes the fuel from the gas tank, mixes it with air from the outside and creates power with it. In a computer, the data request comes in through the mouse and keyboard to the CPU, which requests the data from the Hard Drive, receives it in RAM, does the work it needs to the data in RAM, then sends it back to the Hard Disk when the requests for change to the data cease.

This is why it is so critical that you be aware of what processes are running on a computer before you pull the power. If there is data in RAM when you pull the plug that data is immediately lost. You must power down gracefully for the system to return the updated or changed data to the hard drive before shutting down.

It would be like a sudden clog in your fuel line. The engine stops suddenly and all the fuel in the fuel line is sucked out in the process, then it's gone, and the line is empty. Even if you took the line off and tried to look through it for the fuel, it's already gone. RAM is just a hose. Once it's empty, it's empty, and no amount of playing with it will put what flowed out of it back in.

Expansion cards in a computer allow it to perform functions not built into the motherboard, or better than the functions built into the motherboard. For instance, in our car analogy, an expansion card might be that fancy stereo system you replaced the stock stereo with [Sound Card], or digital light-up gauges in the dashboard [Video Card], or new leather seats [Upgraded mouse or keyboard], or dual exhaust [upgraded PSU].

The outside control panel on the motherboard allows you to connect the peripherals [monitor, keyboard, mouse, speakers, and microphone] to the system so that you can use them, sort of like replacing the steering wheel, shift knob, window tint, and mirrors on your vehicle:

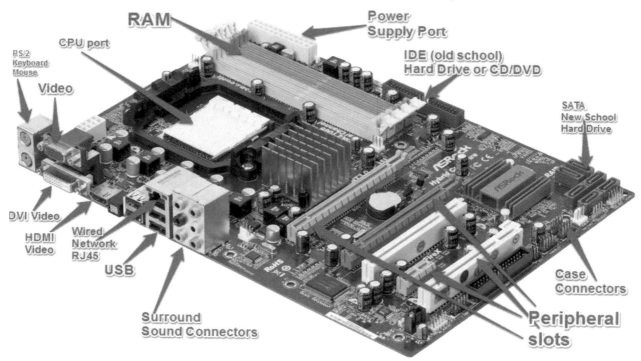

As it boots, the motherboard directs voltage to the other peripherals in the computer, including the hard drive, CD/DVD Drive, and all peripheral ports that are needed to receive input to the motherboard.

The hard disk is segmented or "partitioned" by the operating system into several divisions of data. The very first part of the system is known as the MBR [Master Boot Record] and contains basic instructions that tell the motherboard what size, type, and power requirements the hard drive has, and then directs the motherboard to access each peripheral in a specific order.

The hard disk then instructs the system to allow the commands in the next sector to load in order. This is where the Operating System (Windows, Linux, Apple OS) resides, and it needs all the hardware devices to be warmed up and to have power before it begins to load software instructions in order.

The Operating System looks for the keyboard, mouse, network and video chip (if on the motherboard) or card, RAM, CPU, sound card, CD/DVD drive, and anything else it needs to receive input, and send output to the user.

Also, in a computer, all data is ROM [Read Only Memory] when stored on the hard drive, and can only be modified while in RAM, so think of it just like in a car. You can't burn the gas to go anywhere while it's in the tank, it has to pass through the fuel line to reach the carburetor.

The same is true with your computer. If you have a huge hard drive and a fast CPU, but only 2 gigabytes of RAM, you will constantly be waiting for the system to process your requests. But if you replace that 2 gigabytes with 16 gigabytes of RAM, you will see a HUGE speed upgrade because your fuel line is huge now and the gas can flow freely from your hard drive to your CPU as soon as you request it.

Some computer hard drives can be removable, and some other types of storage media can be as well. Portable devices use Memory Cards to store their data, and they can be quite small, but contain the equivalent to truckloads of paper documents or pictures (data.) When you first turn the power on in a computer, electricity flows to the PSU which converts the 110AC from your house current to DC for the motherboard.

The Motherboard receives the power signal and activates the BIOS, or Basic Input/Output System, which is a series of firmware (software burned directly onto a chip instead of swapped in and out via RAM) instructions that tell the motherboard what it is, how to operate, what language to display, what security functions to use, which input/output ports to operate, and in what order, and what device to access first when "booting".

The user begins seeing data on the screen as soon as the BIOS begins, usually, depending on the settings. Sometimes they only see a system logo, and then commands and/or graphics display as the system "boots" into the Operating System and prepares to provide programming and services to the user.

Computer resources are assigned priority by their function. You want to see things on your screen quickly, so video resources are given "high" priority. You don't really care whether the backup that goes on in the background is running or not, as long as it runs, so it is given "low" priority.

This means that things appear quickly when you click on your word document and the backup running in the background pauses while you are playing World of Warcraft [WOW] so that the video card resources can be dedicated to providing you "seamless" video.

If your backup was given priority, it would run quickly and your WOW screens would jerk, stall, pause, and cause you to get killed a lot.

That said, if you see a data packet travelling the Target's system and can't figure out where it is coming from, you can use a MAC Address lookup service to try and figure it out. Try this for fun:

Open a command prompt on your computer [Start, Run, type command.exe, hit enter] and a black old-school DOS (Disk Operating System, not Denial of Service) type window will appear with a blinking cursor. Type **Ipconfig /all** and hit enter.

31

Introduction to Tactical Hacking: A Guide for Law Enforcement

A bunch of completely worthless numbers will come up on the screen that describe in detail all of the inner workings of your **I**nternet **P**rotocol **CONFIG**uration.

On my screen I see that under each network device there are a series of informational subsets. Each contains information you could use to troubleshoot your network, or to better understand it. But let's focus on the line underneath the label "Wireless LAN Adapter Wi-Fi:" This contains information including a "Physical Address" label with the MAC address of the Wi-Fi card listed as FC-F8-AE-E5-01-5A.

I can use a website to look up the MAC address and find out a little more about the hardware being used. By going to the website at http://www.whatsmyip.org/mac-address-lookup/ and entering my MAC address of FC-F8-AE-E5-01-5A I learned that it is registered to"Intel Corporate", which tells me that the network card I'm using for my Wi-Fi is an Intel chipset. That isn't a lot of information to go on, and it isn't likely to identify my particular card or computer but it does help us identify network transmissions going to and from our target once we properly identify that.

A MAC address is not as unique as a serial number, but it's close, and if you've narrowed down your target to one of two computers, and one is an Apple device, you can be pretty certain it doesn't have any Intel chips in it, though I suppose it might be possible, particularly if they are using an external network card made with Intel parts.

The other information I can glean from the IPConfig info is that the Wi-Fi card is currently not connected to a network, and that it is capable of dual band Wireless AC, which means if I were serving a search warrant later on my target, I would be looking for an AC router, which are fairly new and fairly expensive, but they also have the ability to provide Wi-Fi services, and be backward compatible to many different types of networking devices (Wireless B, G, N, and sometimes A), and have a fairly large coverage area.

Just as a side note, look at the DHCPv6 Client DUID number on the IPConfig window as well as the IPv4 address. You can see how much longer and more complicated the IPv6 address is than the IPv4 address.

All of this information is valuable to assist us in determining the source of network data we are looking at later, when we get into sniffing network traffic, and need to try and verify that we are looking at only our target's data.

This is why if you "shim the stack" at the network layer, you can watch every data packet travelling to and from your Target computer, but it will be in a format designed for a computer to read it, not a person. It goes back up the same stack on its way to the server you fired it at in the first place.

You can also "shim the stack" at the network router level by attaching a sniffer to the "Span Port" on a physical network router farther up the chain of routers in the routing mechanism. This is how the NSA and other three letter agencies do it. They move up the chain of routers closer to the "Backbone," which is the very fastest portion of the Internet that moves all data in a country, and plug a very very fast processing system into the Span Port, which aggregates [monitors, collects, observes] all of the traffic passing by it, and they apply sniffing technologies at that level.

We use the applications in our Kali Laptop or our PwnPad to read and interpret these signals on a much smaller level, and after a little practice with Wireshark and some of the traffic that travels a network, you will quickly realize just how much data passes across even the smallest and most insignificant network.

Chapter 4: Building a Tactical Hacking Lab

Workstations are not complicated beasts. Everyone has a favorite configuration, whether they concentrate all of their money on CPU ability or RAM, but the key goal is to provide the computer with enough processing power and RAM to be able to handle the assigned tasks.

Ask your IT colleagues around the station if they have spare computers lying around. Tell them it is not for personal use, that you will be testing out software and hardware for use in department activities only. Place these requests in writing as well, ensuring you have a record of permission from the department and that you will obtain equipment in good working order.

Tell them you will install the operating systems yourself and will not be connecting these systems to any departmental networks, likely ever, but certainly not without consulting with IT first. Remember, some of these tools can do damage to machines and networks, so you need to AIRGAP your network. With AIRGAP, you create an actual gap between all of your computer systems in your lab and any potential departmental equipment or networks. Even if you are using Wi-Fi, make sure there is a "Signal Gap" between your network and the department network, if there is one. When you run the Wi-Fi scanning and enumeration tools like AirCrack and Fern, they list all available nearby wireless networks.

When you run these tools, you will notice that not only is the name of the Wi-Fi network nearby listed, along with the strength of signal, but also the channel that it is using. If you see your department Wi-Fi using channel 2, look for another channel that is either very weak, or not listed at all. If you see that channels 7-10 do not appear to be in use select one of those.

Putting your Wi-Fi on Channel 8, when your department uses Channel 2, makes it highly unlikely you will cause any interference or bleed-over onto their Wi-Fi setup. I will show you how I built my first lab workstation while setting up the PwnPad in Chapter 6. During that installation, I used an Asus workstation and installed Ubuntu 14.04. During the installation, Ubuntu recognized that I already had a working Windows 7 installation on my hard disk, so it allowed me to dual-boot the system also.

When I booted the laptop I built Chapter 6 I was presented with the screen below:

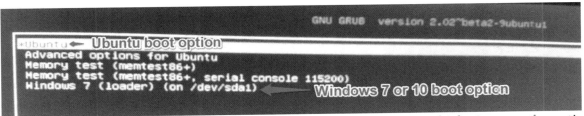

As you can see, Ubuntu installed the GNU Grub bootloader system, which gives me the option to boot into either Ubuntu or Windows 7 every time. One option is to also add Kali Linux to this existing computer, but that would create a triple boot loader situation, and I don't want to use up the rest of my hard disk that way for two reasons: 1. If I load three operating systems on one hard disk, I can only use the tools on each of the operating system one at a time. That is, if I want to run a tool in windows and a tool in Kali, I have to pick one; I can't run both at the same time. 2. If I'm using Kali and I find something that I need to parse further, and the best tool to do that is inside Windows, I have to reboot into Windows to continue working, which stops what I'm already doing.

I use several different computers with different configurations so that I don't have this problem.

Introduction to Tactical Hacking: A Guide for Law Enforcement

My portable systems are all laptops, but my lab systems are not going to be carried from place to place, so I can build them out of workstations and desktop computers, and even older re-purposed servers that my department may have lying around that aren't being used anymore.

I have Windows 7 running on two newer workstations with larger hard drives and more RAM because Windows system files and memory requirement are significantly higher than Linux's. Windows 8 is running on two workstations as well, though I don't have much use for them at this particular moment because no one has written any decent tools for Windows 8. It just isn't popular with developers. The Hackers are certainly enjoying writing viruses for it however.

Ubuntu Linux and Kali Linux are running on several laptops, workstations, and portable tablets [Kindle Fire, Blackberry Playbook, Samsung Galaxy] because they are much more useful for portability. In reality, though, you can only efficiently run one Linux tool at a time on a tablet. They just don't have the processing ability or memory to handle more. Of course, if you have the money, you can purchase tablets with plenty of RAM and space on board, and that will make your portable jobs a lot easier, but don't expect dual processes like Cellular and WIFI to run simultaneously very well on a tablet.

Most of the tools developed for the wireless world were built in Android and Linux because there are so many things purpose-built to be addressable in those languages. The current hardware manufacturing systems have really allowed programmers and developers to write code capable of fully utilizing the hardware of all types of wireless tools, from Wi-Fi to NFC (Near Field Communications) to Bluetooth, the chipset manufacturers leave gaping holes in the API's for the android and Linux developers to access and address commands to, with their software tools.

Learn as much as you can about what other people are using because you will be trying at some point to access other people's machines, devices, even systems. The more you understand about what is available and being used in the field, the more successful you will be. For instance, when Comcast comes out with a new cable box that offers Wi-Fi connectivity, learn how it works. This Wi-Fi system may offer you access to the Target's Wi-Fi network if there is an available exploit. The more you learn about how the different vendors multimedia offerings work, the better off you will be.

Ask your department to purchase a complete entertainment system similar to what AT&T pushes to their clients. Ask AT&T if you can attend their employee training about the system installation and configuration. As long as it is for legitimate government use, they may just invite you to attend.

Install a full Wi-Fi network in your lab. Pick different routers and switches and install those as well. Try as many different pieces of equipment as you can, because you never know what systems your target will be employing when you get there.

The use of servers in your lab are usually based on a financial decision. They can be repurposed older workstations if you just need a place to plug in a bunch of Terabytes of hard drives to store backup and evidence images. But if they will be running brute force hacking tools or trying to crack encryption for you, they need as many processors as the motherboard can handle and as much RAM as you can afford.

Brand of server or workstation is not nearly as important as operating system and hardware base. By hardware base I mean if you are going to use Kali Linux as your workstation operating system, you need to verify that the hardware you are purchasing, or repurposing, is compatible with their requirements.

Faraday Bags

Faraday bags and cages get a lot of publicity because they sound cool and secret. They aren't. All a Faraday bag or cage does is use components to prevent "leakage" of information because Faraday discovered that, "Any change in the magnetic environment of a coil of wire will cause a voltage (emf) to be "induced" in the coil. No matter how the change is produced, the voltage will be generated. The change could be produced by changing the magnetic field strength, moving a magnet toward or away from the coil, moving the coil into or out of the magnetic field, rotating the coil relative to the magnet, etc."[3]

Someone can see what you are doing from a distance, access your computer, read, copy, and change your data, as long as they can get close enough to the device your information is stored on. How does that apply to us? Well, most of the time it has to do with protecting cellular and other portable devices from being remotely wiped by the suspect, or a friend of the suspect, you seized it from. A Faraday bag is constructed of specially woven metal threads that prevent electronic signals from leaving or entering the bag, preventing the electronic device inside the bag from being remotely controlled, commanded, or configured.

Today's modern smartphones are usually based on the Apple iPhone or Android platform, and both of these types of devices have remote wipe and lock capabilities that, if activated by the suspect or someone friendly to the suspect, could either completely block your access to the device, or wipe it clean to the point where any evidence that was on the phone when you seized it, is either corrupted, deleted, or replaced with non-evidence data that no longer relates to your case.

Additionally, you need to be worried about direct access to the device via short-range network communication protocols like Bluetooth and Wi-Fi. You need to prevent outside access to the device via these avenues, while being able to use them to access the device yourself if necessary.

When you seize a device like a cellular phone, that has network access either by the cellular data network, or by Wi-Fi or Bluetooth, you want to work with the device to capture, copy, and protect any data of evidentiary value that is contained within it. However, because you can access it yourself via cellular data, Wi-Fi or Bluetooth, or NFC networking, you may not want to place the device inside a Faraday bag as nothing will get in or out.

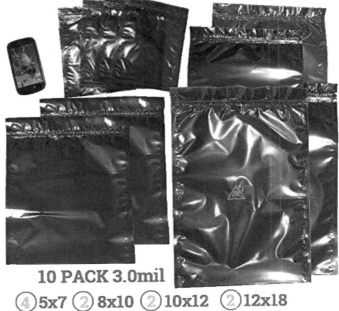

Figure 4: A Pack of Faraday bags, which are used to prevent data wiping on small devices such as cellular phones.

Unless you regularly engage high ranking members of the cartel with specialized data on their cellular phone, you are unlikely to need to protect the phone longer than necessary to use a Cellebrite type device to "dump" it. A Faraday bag [See Figure 4] would do fine to protect it from remote wiping until you are done with your investigation. They are available to

---

[3] http://hyperphysics.phy-astr.gsu.edu/hbase/electric/farlaw.html

Introduction to Tactical Hacking: A Guide for Law Enforcement

purchase on Amazon and at other vendors. Make sure whatever you purchase for use in your lab you test yourself first, as you may be required to testify that it does what you say it does.

When working on larger machines with very sensitive data on them for long periods of time, you may need to find a nearby scientific lab with Faraday Shielding, because building one of your own could cost in the hundreds of thousands of dollars. Try to arrange for this ahead of time so that you aren't scrambling around wasting precious minutes in an important investigation.

You also need to be worried about your lab design for use of wireless devices, either to test, or actually use potentially damaging, or illegal wireless software and hardware. For instance, if you are using a wireless scanning software to check the device you have seized for any potential access points, you are actively probing the network it is using for vulnerabilities. If that scanning were to escape your lab, it could potentially end up scanning any nearby wireless devices for vulnerabilities, and in some cases, with some software, actively trying to exploit that access to gain control of the device.

While that may be okay in the lab, and you may have a search warrant or other legal reason to use the software and access the device, you need to make certain you have control over the signals you are sending and don't accidentally compromise or exploit other nearby devices, particularly your own or your employers.

Enumeration

Enumeration means "establish the number of" and, in computer parlance, loosely relates to running a query across a spectrum to determine how many devices it holds. Then a second query is run against the devices discovered in an attempt to get them to respond, which helps identify what and where the device is.

Electronic enumeration and querying of devices is an art form. When locating devices on a network, I am careful to avoid a subnet or nearby networks. It does me no good to be scanning devices that have nothing to do with my target.

The basic requirements of a penetration testing lab include the ability to build, modify, configure, and rapidly change multiple types of wired and wireless networks, as many local client workstations or virtual machines as you can afford/manage, and a few test boxes that are unprotected and can be attacked.

For your wired network you will need networking cables, plugs for each end of each cable, various sizes, speeds, and types of network Switches, Hubs, and other interconnecting devices [including patch cables and other specialized cables for connecting routers and switches together rather than to a computer].

For your wireless network you will need various types, speeds, and configurations of wireless routers, switches, modems, hubs, print servers, Bluetooth devices for sharing, sending and receiving, and terminating or jamming signals (be careful with this as it is a Federal crime to jam legitimate spectrum users,) various sizes and types of receiving and sending equipment and antenna's, including the original HAM Radio equipment if you really want to get deep in the woods.

It is also important to check compatible wireless networks are configured in such a way that they will not interference with each other or contaminate any nearby wireless resources. Do this by activating one wireless network at a time, or verify that each is on a separate radio channel, far enough removed on the spectrum from other nearby signals as to not cause interference.

Designate your two most robust computer systems to be your attacker and target machines. This will allow you to replicate your eventual live target's configuration and decide how best to attack it. It will also allow you to test new tools and configurations for your systems with a system that will most quickly complete your tasks. Testing against your high powered target machine will tell you which items of malware could cause your machines problems if the target gets a chance to launch them back across whatever computer channels you open.

Chapter 4: Building a Tactical Hacking Lab

Load your target machine with prebuilt vulnerable configurations and then "image" [take a digital copy and store it somewhere safe] it to make restoring it to the exact condition you built it in much more quick and effective, and ensure you are always starting with a "clean" or at least "known good" state when testing or attacking.

In the lab you have more space and resources available to account for different types of media and technology you may come across, whether from your Target directly, or other sources. Installing different types of media read/write technology, including card readers that can read many different types of memory cards you may encounter in cellular phones, cameras, tablets, and devices with the ability to read/write data locally. These devices usually use a USB cable or other connector and can be used locally or with a laptop or other portable device. You can mount and access multiple types of hard drives, including the older IDE and SCSI/SAS drives, the newer SATA, and the latest SSD hard drive types.

Chapter 5: Tactical Hacking Field Platforms

Building a Tactical Hacking platform for use in the field or that can be moved around inside a structure like a correctional facility will be essentially based on deciding where you will be placed in the field and what types of technology you will need to have available to you.

For instance, if you are deploying in a Lenco Bearcat for the purpose of using it as a command post, you might have power and internet access far superior to that of a regular patrol vehicle, but far inferior to what you might have in a fifth wheel trailer command post purpose built with workstations and cellular, landline, and high speed internet access, and a generator.

If you are moving the device around from place to place inside a correctional facility, power, latency, and concealment options will be an issue for you, as well as physical obstructions to the network, your device, and your targets.

From a technical standpoint, you will also need to decide what capabilities you want to have available to you right from the beginning of the incident. If you want to have access to a physical network with multiple workstations and the ability to sniff Wi-Fi, Bluetooth, cellular, and wired network packets all simultaneously, a Pwnphone or Pwnpad won't be the best resource. Even a Kali Laptop build will not likely be able to handle all of these simultaneously, so pick your equipment based on where and how you will be deploying it.

I suggest you start with a Kali Linux laptop because they are robust, easy to build, and will provide you with an easy introduction into the Linux operating system and Kali's powerful tools. This book is designed to provide you with money-saving options so we are going to talk about how to re-purpose an older laptop that may be lying around your department after having languished for several years when someone in a higher pay grade decided they needed an upgrade.

The easiest way to test out Kali is to download and configure a bootable USB or CD-Rom so that you can play with it on your hardware without actually installing it. This is a good way to test your hardware compatibility, because if your laptop will not run Kali from a CD-Rom or USB drive, you will probably not be able to run it installed on the laptop either. However, Kali will run much slower from the CD-Rom as the program data has to be constantly swapped into and out of the RAM on your laptop, which will result in data bottlenecks and delays, particularly on older, less robust hardware.

That said, the minimum hardware requirements are incredibly low and you will likely be able to boot from a CD-Rom from pretty much any laptop or computer made in the last 15 years with an Intel CPU.

Use your trusty working windows or Linux or apple computer to go to www.kali.org and follow the instructions for your hardware to ensure you download the correct image for your system and hardware. I will, however, suggest to you that you carefully consider other installation options if you are trying to have an "all-in-one" approach to deploying Kali. For instance, if you are limited on space but have a Windows based computer already available, running VMWare or Virtual Box Guest with the preconfigured VMWare or VirtualBox images already designed by the Kali distribution team may be an excellent way to move back and forth between the scans and information gathering processes in Kali while using the Windows side of the computer for other tasks.

You will have configuration challenges with this setup as well, however, as each program running on your computer takes resources away from the others, and if your system becomes unstable or is underpowered, you run the risk of having created a single point of failure.

Windows also offers a very limited, but powerful set of tools for researching a device already in your possession, in a forensically sound environment called the Windows Forensic Environment "WinFE" for short. This tool comes in various bootable configurations including CD-Rom, DVD, USB, or potentially Network based configurations, but you would really need to know your network stuff to be able to remotely push this configuration to a target machine.

For those of you with a masochistic bend toward policy and procedure absorption, OWASP (Open Web Application Security Project), OSSTMM (Open Source Security Testing Methodology Manual), and ISO 27001 (Auditing Standards surrounding protection mechanisms and computer postmortem details) are excellent sources for exceedingly complex and overly careful lab building techniques.

For the rest of us, building a Kali based laptop can be done in many different ways. Until you have all the nuances of disk partitioning and multi-boot platforms down really, really good, you should stick with a basic, dedicated build, single system for your Kali laptop.

I am going to build two laptops for this book, a dual-boot Windows/Kali Linux with a four-year-old Asus U46E because that's what I have handy, and a single boot kali laptop with an IBM Thinkpad T40, which is more like nine years old and decidedly less robust.

Kali Linux Installation Procedure:

Download the ISO file for the most recent Kali Linux Build and burn it to CD-Rom. Go to www.kali.org on a computer that has the ability to burn DVD's. The Kali Linux build is too big to be put onto a CD-Rom any longer, so a computer with a DVD burner is preferred. Once you get to the website click on the "Downloads" tab at the top of the webpage.

Once at the Downloads page, you have several options. In the bottom right corner of the page you will find some very helpful links about Kali Linux, so if you get lost or need other suggestions for different types of builds than I am describing here, try there first.

You will need to determine whether your hardware will support a 32 bit or a 64 bit software installation. The difference between the two is basically hardware capable of handling 64 bits of data at a time will process the software through its RAM much faster than a machine that can only handle 32 bits of data at a time. This is a hardware configuration that cannot be changed, so no use grousing about it if your hardware will not support 64 bit software.
If the machine you are going to be building on already has Windows software installed and it will boot, you will have a much faster time of figuring this out, but the bottom line is, if you can't determine for certain which your computer will support, download the 32 bit Kali build, as it's unlikely you will be using a computer so old it can't handle at least that.   If you can boot into Windows, go to Control Panel, then the System tab and just read the screen. Somewhere on there you are likely to see the words "32 Bit" or "64 Bit."

To Begin Installation:

To start your installation, boot with your chosen installation medium. You should be greeted with the Kali Boot screen. Choose either Graphical or Text-Mode install. In this example, we chose a GUI install.

The GUI option means you are presented with pictures you can click on rather than just a black screen with text scrolling across. You have several options here, and this is a good time to point out to you that if you aren't yet sure whether your hardware (laptop or desktop computer) is compatible with a full installation of the Kali Linux build, this is a good opportunity to find out if Kali is compatible.

Choose the "Live (Forensic Mode)" or the "Live (amd64)" mode and the system will move forward booting into the entire Kali Linux system. Once you have checked that it boots completely and works properly on your hardware, come back to this screen and choose the Graphical Install option to complete installation of the Kali Linux build to your system.

This is also a good time to point out that if you continue with the installation at this point, you will **lose everything on the hard disk of the machine you are installing to.** If this is not going to

Introduction to Tactical Hacking: A Guide for Law Enforcement

be a dedicated Kali Linux built box, you need to back out now, you are in danger of erasing the entire system.

You can also decide at this time to take a brand new hard disk and install it in the laptop or workstation and install Kali on that. This will preserve the existing hard disk and installations of other operating systems you may have on it already. Simply remove the existing hard disk and replace it with a fresh new one. You may actually be questioned on the stand about that at some point, so it is best, if feasible, to be building your system from a hard disk that you took out of the brand new OEM packaging yourself.

This will prevent the Defense that the information you gathered against the Target during your tactical incident was actually "leftover remnants" from a corrupt or previously installed hard disk.

You can usually defeat this type of argument by stating that you installed the system to a fresh hard disk you opened yourself after purchasing it off the shelf from a reputable computer company, however, if you are using a "used" hard disk that does not have anything valuable on it that you need to keep for any reason, you may want to consider "zeroing it out", or using a software package like Eraser (http://sourceforge.net/projects/eraser/) to create a bootable hard disk wiper with a full suite of options to allow you to verify that any data existing on the drive before you used Eraser on it has been obliterated to a point it would be practically impossible for the drive to have any leftover data remnants.

It has been generally accepted that overwriting every sector of the hard drive accessible with randomized data, like the Eraser program does, is considered "MILSPEC" or to military specifications, and if it's good enough for the military to consider it securely wiped, you should be able to successfully argue that you've done your due diligence to make any remaining data remnants unlikely to be successfully recovered on purpose, much less accidentally by the tools in the Kali Linux build.

Select your preferred language and then your country location. You will also be prompted to configure your keyboard with the appropriate keymap.

The installer will copy the image to your hard disk, probe your network interfaces, and then prompt you to enter a hostname for your system. In the following example [See Figure 5], "kali" is our hostname.

Figure 5

Chapter 5: Building a Tactical Hacking Field Platform

Domain names are used to help create a directory structure, or to insert a networked device into a network directory structure so unless you really understand networking and are intentionally assigning a domain name, don't put anything in here [See Figure 6], and delete anything that self-populates.

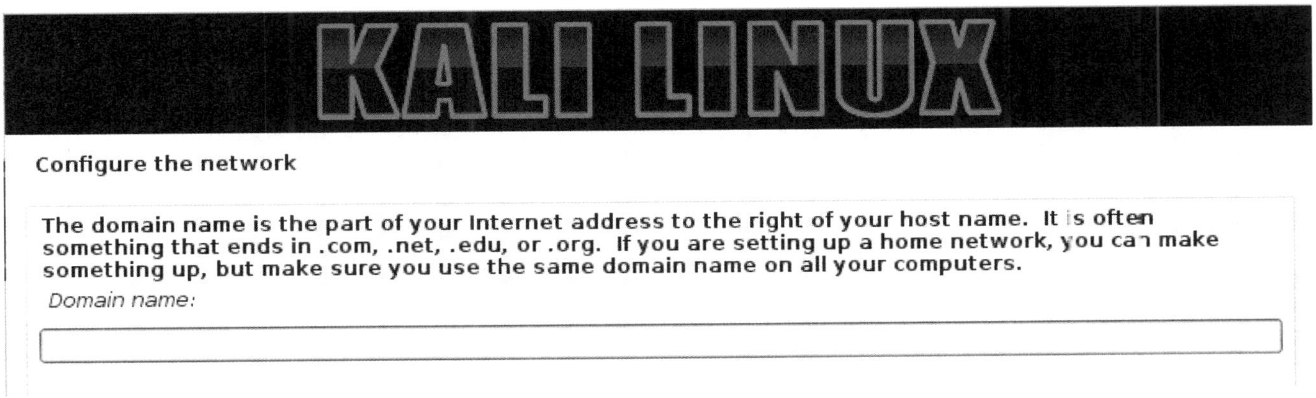

KALI LINUX

Configure the network

The domain name is the part of your Internet address to the right of your host name. It is often something that ends in .com, .net, .edu, or .org. If you are setting up a home network, you can make something up, but make sure you use the same domain name on all your computers.

Domain name:

Figure 6

Next, provide a full name for a non-root user for the system [See Figure 7].

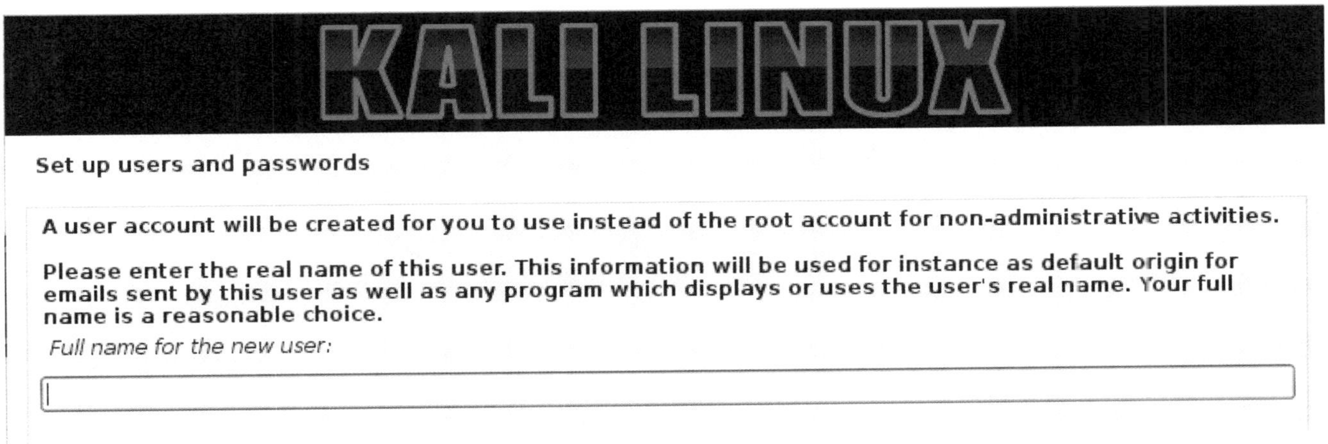

KALI LINUX

Set up users and passwords

A user account will be created for you to use instead of the root account for non-administrative activities.

Please enter the real name of this user. This information will be used for instance as default origin for emails sent by this user as well as any program which displays or uses the user's real name. Your full name is a reasonable choice.

Full name for the new user:

Figure 7

The "Root" user in Linux is like the "Admin" or "Administrator" user in Windows machines. It has "GOD" rights, meaning it can do anything on the machine without escalating any additional privileges.

Root should only be used by someone with the need to make changes to a system that an Administrator would make, and operating as the Root user is generally discouraged because if your system is compromised while you are operating as Root, the person/software that was able to compromise the system will have all the rights and authority of the Root user. This is a bad thing.

So generally, it is recommended that all users only operate under a non-root level account, which is why they are recommending you create a secondary user account. However, because we will be operating as GOD on our systems for the sake of efficiency and speed, this user name and account will only be useful as an identifier for the system, so name it whatever you want. Just remember the name and password you create in case you ever find yourself needing to operate as that user. Print out a label with this information and stick it to the bottom of the machine if you

41

Introduction to Tactical Hacking: A Guide for Law Enforcement

don't have an account management or password management tool like Lastpass (www.lastpass.com) to use for storing all of your account names and passwords.

A default user ID will be created, based on the full name you provided. You can change this if you like. Next, set your time zone. You may not think setting a time zone is important, but, in reality, it can be critical to your testimony in a case later. Many datasets recovered as evidence will be timestamped by the systems they either generated from, passed through, or resided in. It could become critical evidence that a piece of data was recorded with GMT timestamps, and it could help pinpoint a computer user's location.

Researching time zones and the time discrepancies between your particular geographic location and the collected data could indicate the following: 1. You have captured data, originating from a different location, from a local source that was attempting to "spoof" [fake] or 2. Your actual source of the data is in another time zone altogether.

Use your time zone, or GMT by default, to ensure datasets are evaluated accordingly. The following excerpt is from an analysis of the case files used in the Casey Anthony murder trial. Though she was found not guilty in the murder of her daughter, this describes a pivotal piece of evidence the Prosecution used in an attempt to show premeditation by Anthony. Afterward, the Defense presented the same evidence, demonstrating inappropriate skewing of the time stamp data:

*"**Forensic Analysis***

It is a matter of record that our software NetAnalysis (v1.37) was used during the initial examination of this data, and then at a later stage another tool was used. This is, of course, good forensic practice and is often referred to as "dual tool verification".

Within a Mork database, the timestamp information relating to visits are stored as a microsecond count from an epoch of 1st January 1970 at 00:00:00 hours UTC (Universal Coordinated Time). In NetAnalysis v1.37, the forensic examiner had an option to leave the timestamps as they were recorded in the original evidence or to apply a bias to the UTC value to translate it to a local "Standard Time". In this older version, there was no option to present the timestamp as a local value adjusted for DST (Daylight Saving Time). This changed in NetAnalysis v1.50 when a further date column was introduced which presented the examiner with UTC and local times adjusted for DST."[4]

Investigators for the Prosecution tried to correlate the recovered data with local time. As a result, the evidence was so confusing the Defense could argue it was immaterial because the Prosecution had "tampered with" it. Better to leave the data as is.

The installer will now probe your disks and offer you four choices. In our example, we're using the entire disk on our computer and not configuring LVM [logical volume manager]. Experienced users can use the "Manual" partitioning method for more granular configuration options. Do not mess with these settings unless you truly understand what you are doing.

---

[4] http://www.digital-detective.net/digital-evidence-discrepancies-casey-anthony-trial/

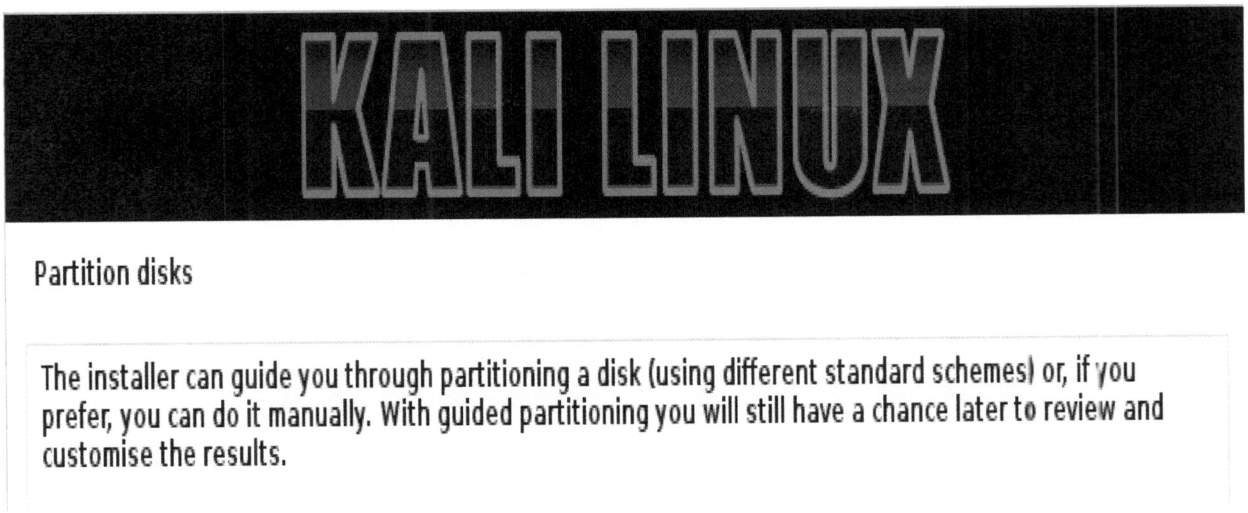

Chapter 5: Building a Tactical Hacking Field Platform

Figure 8

Select the disk to be partitioned [See Figure 8]. Unless multiple disks are listed here, do not change this setting. That said, to prevent additional confusion remove any externally connected hard disks or thumb drives prior to this step to prevent accidentally installing on the wrong drive.

Depending on your needs, you can choose to keep all your files in a single partition — the default — or to have separate partitions for one or more of the top-level directories. If you're not sure which, select "All files in one partition" [See Figure 9]. Some of you may recognize this step if you have ever built a Windows-based machine. Do not be confused by the Drive 0 designation. Unix people believe 0 is a number, and so they set the first addressable hard drive as disk 0.

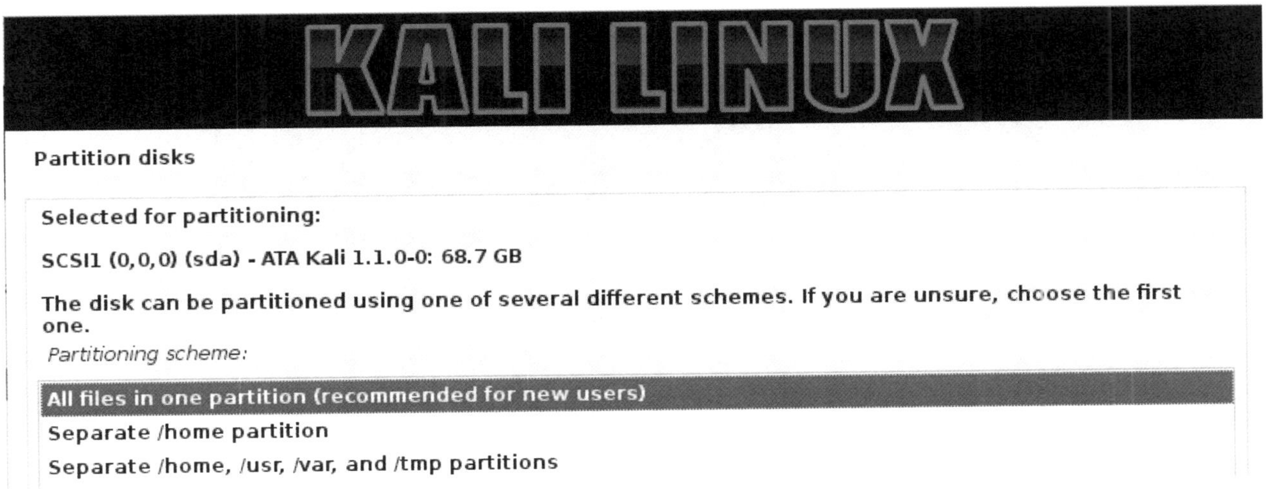

Figure 9

Next, you'll have one last chance to review your disk configuration before the installer makes irreversible changes [See Figure 10]. After you click "Continue," the installer will go to work and you'll have an almost finished installation. Don't change anything here unless you are really sure something is amiss and you completely understand what and why it is.

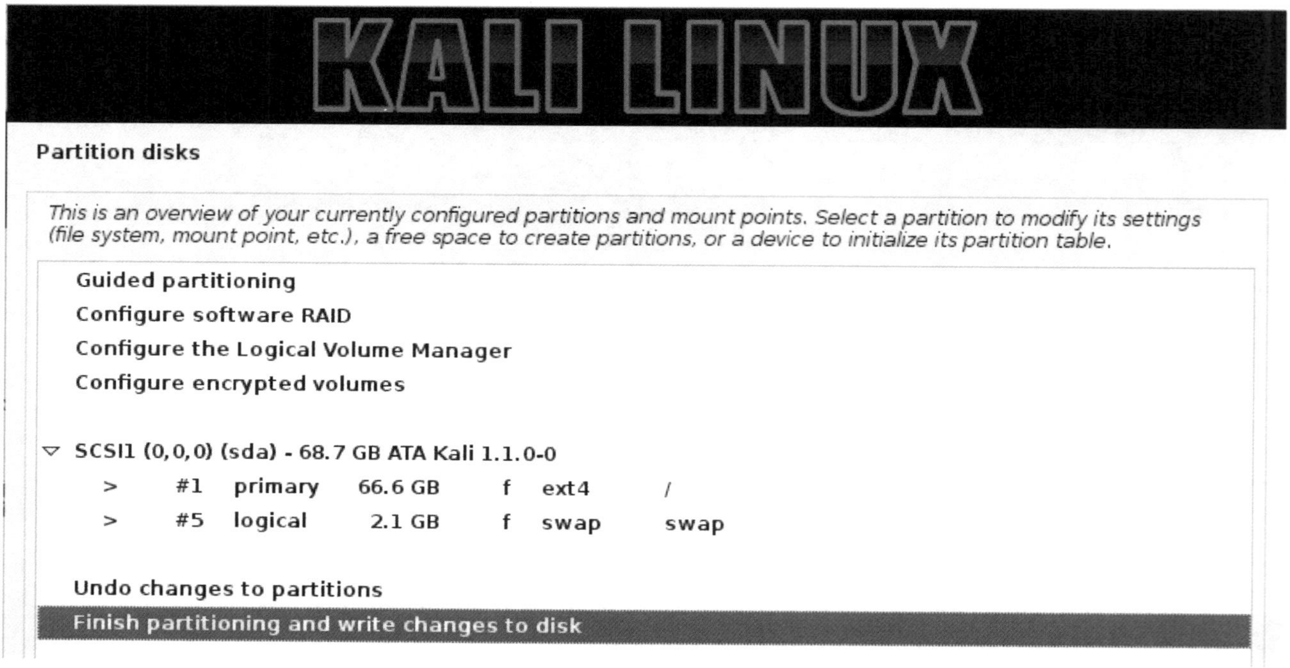

Introduction to Tactical Hacking: A Guide for Law Enforcement

Partition disks

This is an overview of your currently configured partitions and mount points. Select a partition to modify its settings (file system, mount point, etc.), a free space to create partitions, or a device to initialize its partition table.

    Guided partitioning

    Configure software RAID

    Configure the Logical Volume Manager

    Configure encrypted volumes

▽ SCSI1 (0,0,0) (sda) - 68.7 GB ATA Kali 1.1.0-0

    >   #1   primary   66.6 GB   f   ext4   /

    >   #5   logical   2.1 GB   f   swap   swap

    Undo changes to partitions

    Finish partitioning and write changes to disk

Figure 10

Configure network mirrors [See Figure 11]. Kali uses a central repository to distribute applications. You'll need to enter any appropriate proxy information as needed. Don't change anything here and make sure your computer is connected physically to a network with Internet access or you will get an error message. *Note: If you select "NO" in this screen, you will NOT be able to install packages from Kali repositories.*

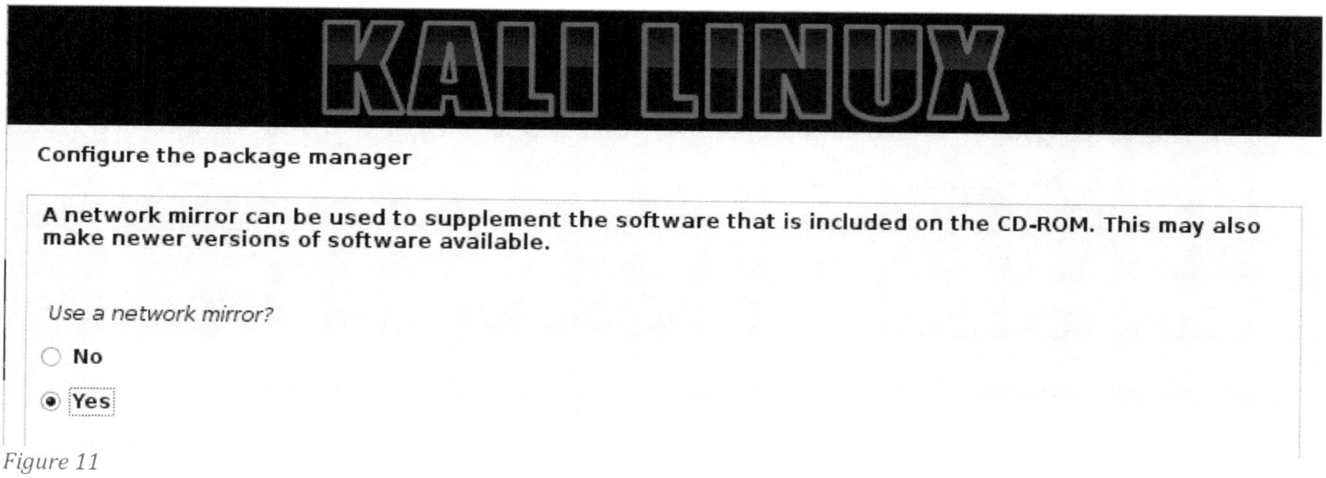

Configure the package manager

A network mirror can be used to supplement the software that is included on the CD-ROM. This may also make newer versions of software available.

Use a network mirror?

○ No

◉ Yes

Figure 11

Chapter 5: Building a Tactical Hacking Field Platform

Next, install GRUB [See Figure 12]. This may result in some confusion. You definitely want GRUB as your boot loader, but it will detect any previously installed operating systems on your computer. Then it will give you an error asking if you want to multi-boot your Kali Linux build. If it was your intention to load more than one Operating System on this system, and you really know what you are doing, move forward. For the rest of us, choose "Yes" and retrace your steps if it doesn't say this is a new installation.

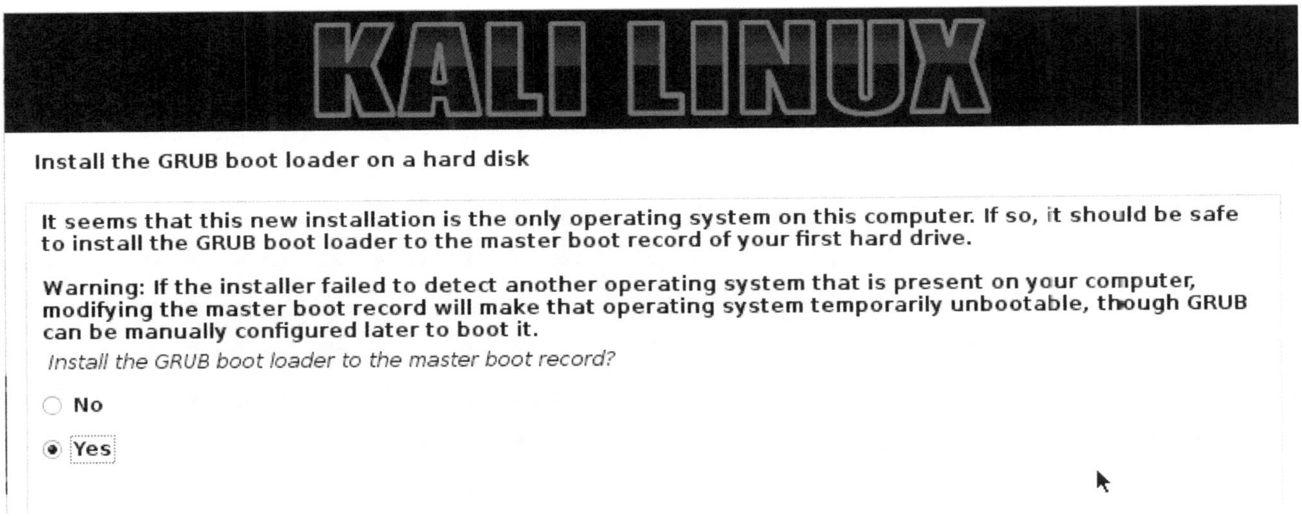

Install the GRUB boot loader on a hard disk

It seems that this new installation is the only operating system on this computer. If so, it should be safe to install the GRUB boot loader to the master boot record of your first hard drive.

Warning: If the installer failed to detect another operating system that is present on your computer, modifying the master boot record will make that operating system temporarily unbootable, though GRUB can be manually configured later to boot it.

Install the GRUB boot loader to the master boot record?

○ No

◉ Yes

Figure 12

Finally, click Continue to reboot into your new Kali installation.

45

Chapter 6: Building a Tactical Hacking Tablet

Kali can also be purpose built directly to a specific portable device like the Google Nexus Tablet in the form of the PwnPad or PwnPhone[5]. However, again, price becomes an issue. In the next section I will describe how I purchased a broken Google Nexus tablet from Craigslist for $100.00, rooted it, and installed the Community Edition of the PwnPad software, turning the tablet into a very effective and extremely powerful penetration testing tool.

This certainly beats thousands of dollars in expenditures to private corps requiring regular and expensive maintenance agreements, but it also requires a good amount of electronics and computer networking understanding, and is not for the faint of heart. Still, it can do everything a $10k commercial device can do, and, in some cases, better.

If you decide to take this on, you will need patience, because the PwnieExpress folks allow their software to be ported for free, but they don't make it easy. You need to start at the Pwnieexpress.com website dedicated to the "Community Edition."[6] For those of you with a budget and no time for a challenge, head on over to https://www.pwnieexpress.com/product/pwn-pad-2014-penetration-testing-tablet/ and purchase it pre-configured for $995.00.

That's actually a great deal, because the devices alone cost close to that, so you are getting all their labor at practically nothing. Plus you get the customer support, and these guys/gals really know their stuff. This also provides you with access to their warranty, training, and support tracks, all of which I highly recommend if you have the budget for it. I started my quest by checking the hardware requirements section through their site. You need to be certain you are acquiring the exact hardware device they request, right down to the exact model number, and this was my first challenge.

I first tried this out after visiting the PwnieExpress booth at DEFCON in Las Vegas. The Google Nexus 7 was fairly new, and ridiculously expensive, priced at around $799. So I checked on my local Craigslist and discovered a listing for one that was too good to be true. A fellow in Mountain View, California had dropped his shortly after purchasing it, cracking the screen severely. Because he didn't pay the insurance on it, and there weren't any aftermarket screens available yet, he was listing it for only $200.

---

[5] https://www.pwnieexpress.com/product/pwn-pad-2014-penetration-testing-tablet/.
[6] https://www.pwnieexpress.com/community/

Chapter 6: Building a Tactical Hacking Tablet

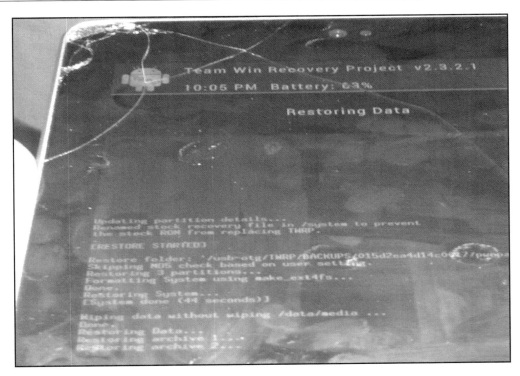

Figure 13

It needed quite a bit of work [See Figure 13], but I could get it to function pretty much as it was. So I got started with this process, downloaded directly from pwnieexpress.com, with their permission. The instruction manual contains a lot of excellent information, but quite a bit assumes knowledge not necessarily in evidence. It starts out with the aptly named "What you'll need"[7] and provides all of the hardware specifications:

- A computer running a Linux-based operating system (Ubuntu 12.04 recommended)

    NOTE: Using a virtual machine is not recommended due to Nexus 7 USB host mode compatibility limitations.

- One of the following Nexus 7 tablet models:

    - The newer (2013) edition Nexus 7 tablet (32GB, Wi-Fi + LTE Mobile data, Model K009) **(RECOMMENDED)**
    - The older (2012) edition Nexus 7 tablet (32GB, Wi-Fi + Mobile data) **(RECOMMENDED)**
    - The older (2012) edition Nexus 7 tablet (32GB, Wi-Fi only)
    - The older (2012) edition Nexus 7 tablet (16GB, Wi-Fi only)

- A micro-USB OTG to USB 2.0 adapter (We recommend: http://www.newegg.com/Product/Product.aspx?Item=9SIA0PG06U1118)

- A TP-Link TL-WN722N USB adapter (for 802.11 wireless pentesting)
- (Optional) A SENA UD100 industrial Bluetooth USB adapter (for Bluetooth pentesting)
- (Optional) A USB-to-Ethernet adapter (for pentesting wired networks)
- (Optional) Velcro for attaching accessories to the back of the Nexus 7

---

[7] http://www.pwnieexpress.com/wp-content/uploads/2015/05/Pwn-Pad-Community-Edition-Factory-Image-Installation-Guide.pdf

Introduction to Tactical Hacking: A Guide for Law Enforcement

Thankfully, they give you the specific make and model numbers of all of the hardware you should have, and often provide a direct web link. I downloaded the package as instructed, but I used a Windows computer to attempt imaging the first time. They don't recommend that, and I soon found out why: It's hard. In my case anyway, it took three tries to even get the image across, but let's take it step by step:

1. Secure broken or slightly damaged Google Nexus 7 with the correct model number.
2. Build a Linux based machine. Unfortunately, it turns out that the Kali Linux build, while based on Ubuntu, is not correctly configured for the installation we need. Instead, go to www.ubuntu.com and download the latest version for desktop. I used Ubuntu 14.04.2 for desktop, and again, choose the 32 bit version if you are not certain that your hardware will support the 64 bit version.
3. Once downloaded, you have to install the Ubuntu operating system on a desktop or laptop. I recommend you either put a different hard disk into your lab laptop, if you are comfortable doing that, or use a different computer all together. This can be a laptop or desktop, your choice. I chose a desktop machine because later in the book we will be building a lab workstation anyway, so why not start now.
4. You need, or at least should, follow the instructions to verify you have the minimum hardware requirements for a desktop or laptop for the version of Ubuntu you download. I downloaded the latest version at the time this book was being written, which was Ubuntu 14.04.
5. I used the same process we used to build the Kali ISO image onto a DVD and downloaded the ISO image, then used IMGBurn to burn the ISO image to a DVD, then booted the DVD in my lab workstation, which I build out of a Asus motherboard with an I5 Intel processor and 16 gigabytes of ram, on a 1 terabyte hard disk. This is super overpowered for what Ubuntu needs, but for a lab workstation this is perfect.
6. Once I booted the new machine, I chose F2 to go into the Bios and set the boot order to boot from the DVD drive first, then I rebooted with the DVD of the Ubuntu 14.04 ISO in the DVD drive. The system boots from the DVD when you do this, I and got this page:

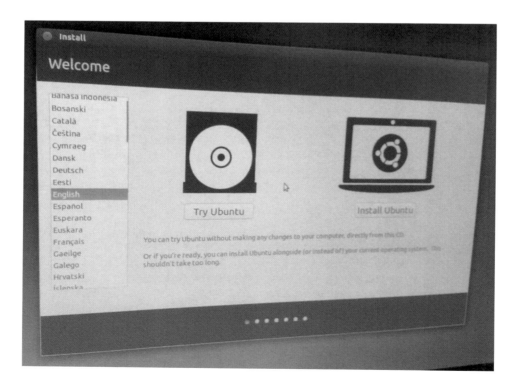

My lab workstation detected several of my local networks. I chose the appropriate Wi-Fi network and continued the installation. It told me to verify I had at least a minimum available hard disk space and was connected to the Internet. Then it told me that it would download updates while installing. I clicked "Continue:"

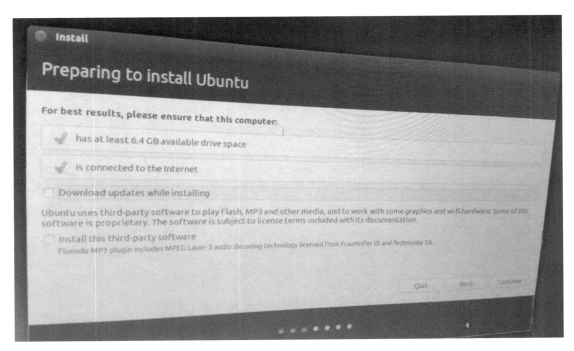

This hard drive already had Windows 7 installed on it, so I decided to keep that, as I might need it on my lab workstation anyway, so I left it selected to install Ubuntu alongside Windows 7 and clicked "Continue:"

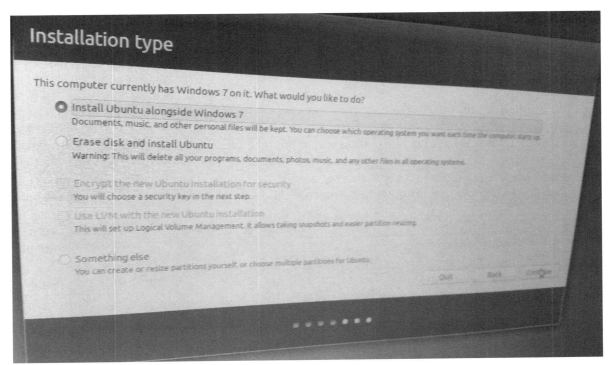

Introduction to Tactical Hacking: A Guide for Law Enforcement

Ubuntu detected the current needs of my Windows 7 installation and offered to partition my hard drive so that 684.1 GB remained dedicated to the Windows 7 installation, and 316 GB would be dedicated to the new Ubuntu installation. Since the initial page stated that I only needed 6.4 GB free on my hard disk to properly install Ubuntu, 316 GB should be more than enough, and would leave me with some breathing room as well. I clicked "Install Now:"

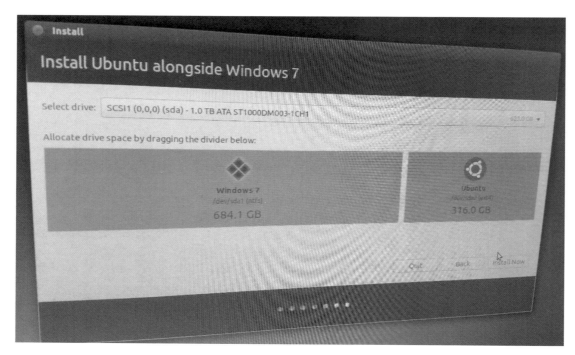

Ubuntu then warned me that the changes to my partition size [the amount of the hard drive dedicated to Windows 7 and the amount dedicated to Ubuntu] would be permanently assigned, and I could not change it. I'm familiar with this warning, and, although I have never seen it take more than 5 minutes, it might take a while. I selected "Continue" and got another "check" screen designed to scare me into not making the changes.

I decided to take their advice and just verified that my correct hard disk was listed at the top. Check by make, model, size, or serial if you know it. If this is the only hard disk in the system, click "Continue."

Ten seconds later they wanted to know what part of the world I was in. This is important because certain types of software and system drivers rely on world time clocks. These clocks synchronize over the Internet via Network Time Protocol [NTP] servers, which are in service to synchronize data across the Internet with machines that need that level of accuracy. I'm on the West Coast of the United States so I left it as is.

After that, I saw the usual language selections, and then the login page. I chose this as a lab system and gave it a user name and password that I wanted it to have for my lab. I recommend you make this something easy to remember and scalable. Remember, you may have to testify later that you had a password that was difficult to guess, so it is unlikely your machine was compromised and the suspect's information, therefore, compromised.

I also decided to have the system encrypt my home folder. Why? Because Ubuntu has the unique ability to encrypt and de-encrypt your system folders "on the fly," making it difficult, if not impossible, for an intruder to gather anything from them.

Chapter 6: Building a Tactical Hacking Tablet

You may find entire functions of the Operating System that simply will not function. Have no fear, run the latest updates, and if you are feeling contributory, report the error so that volunteers can correct it in the future. Upon completion of installation, it will ask you to restart the computer to use the new installation. Click "Restart Now." Upon rebooting the now dual-boot workstation, you will see the following screen:

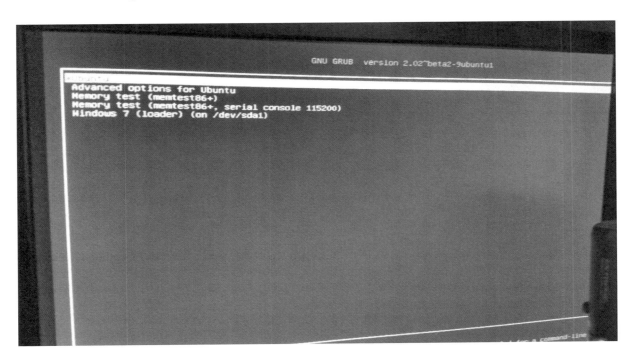

Notice you have the option of allowing it to just continue booting into Ubuntu, or selecting Windows 7 from the boot loader if you need to load on that side of the computer.

Now we can load the installer for our PwnPad:
1. Download the installation package. This is not as easy as it sounds. Turns out the link in their Installation Guide, https://www.pwnieexpress.com/support/downloads/ is broken. You have to actually click on the Community page we were on earlier, then just scroll down to the packages, but make sure you choose the PwnPad version, not the PwnPhone version. I downloaded the one for the 2013 Nexus 7, file name PwnPad-2013_image tar.xz, and it was 1.1 gigabytes in size, which is not small, so it took a little while [about 35 minutes] on my Kali Linux laptop, but it worked. The most important part of this step is to make sure you know exactly where on your Kali Laptop you are downloading the package, as you can get very confused trying to find things in command line mode in Linux. They use very different commands than Windows boxes do.
2. Extract the installation package after downloading it. This can get confusing, but only if you aren't paying attention. If you follow directions, and download the package on the Kali laptop, you will save yourself a lot of heartache. I can't tell you how long it took me to figure out that typing Linux commands on a Linux laptop will return errors if you downloaded the installation package on your Windows machine next to it.
3. So, they make it sound so easy to just "Open Terminal and change to the directory where the PwnPad installation package is located," but if you are new to Linux like me, that isn't as easy as it sounds.

Introduction to Tactical Hacking: A Guide for Law Enforcement

4. "Open Terminal" means starting a program inside Linux called Terminal. This program doesn't advertise itself, and is very difficult to find. You have to look for it here:

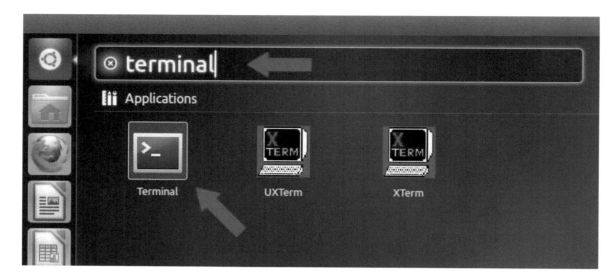

5. Once you click on it and it opens up, then you have to figure out where you are, and how to find the package you just downloaded. Do this by figuring out where you are first. Type "LS" and hit enter. If you are lucky, you are on the Desktop, which will appear at the top of the screen, in blue, and you can see the pwnpad-2013_image.tar.xz right below it in red:

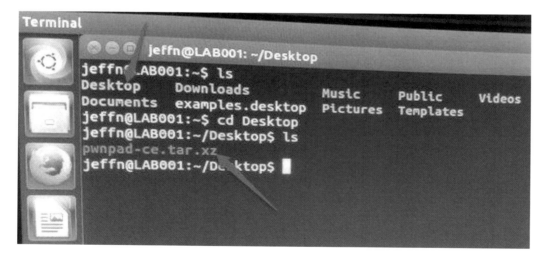

6. If not, try CD Desktop and see if that helps. Be aware here though, that Linux is completely case dependent. So when you type cd Desktop, you have to capitalize the 'D' in Desktop, or it will tell you nothing, or return an error. Once you see Desktop in Blue, type cd Desktop exactly as it appears on the screen, then type LS and you should see your download package:

Chapter 6: Building a Tactical Hacking Tablet

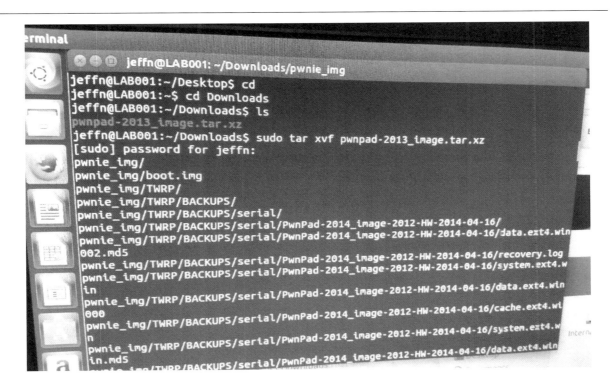

Introduction to Tactical Hacking: A Guide for Law Enforcement

7. Now you are at the right location, you can follow the commands listed below:[8]

Extract the package & run the installer script

Note: All below instructions assume you're using a Debian Linux-based host computer (Ubuntu 12.04 recommended). Using a virtual machine is <u>not</u> recommended due to Nexus 7 USB host mode compatibility limitations.

1. Open Terminal and change to the directory where the Pwn Pad installation package is located.
2. Next, add the required repository and install the "*adb*" and "*fastboot*" packages onto your Linux host computer by typing the following lines and pressing Enter after each line.

   ```
   $ sudo add-apt-repository ppa:nilarimogard/webupd8
   $ sudo apt-get update
   $ sudo apt-get install android-tools-adb android-tools-fastboot
   ```

3. Untar the Pwn Pad installation package downloaded by typing the following and press Enter. Note the process of "untarring" the package may takes several minutes to complete.

   ```
   $ sudo tar xvf pwnpad-*.tar.xz
   ```

4. Next, change directories and make the script executable by typing the following lines and pressing Enter after each line.

   ```
   $ cd pwnie_img/
   $ sudo chmod +x imagev2.sh
   ```

5. Connect the Nexus 7 tablet to the host computer using the stock Nexus 7 micro-USB cable. Do NOT use any USB extension cables, USB hubs, or any additional adapters.
6. Hold the Nexus 7 power and volume-down buttons simultaneously to boot into Fastboot mode.
7. Once Fastboot appears on the screen of the Nexus 7, it is within Terminal on the host computer, type the following line and press Enter to initialize the adb server:

   ```
   $ sudo adb start-server
   ```

8. Now, run the Pwn Pad image installation script by typing the following line and pressing Enter:

   ```
   $ sudo ./imagev2.sh
   ```

9. Follow the onscreen step-by-step instructions from the script.

   Notes:
   a. Answer "Yes" if prompted to install additional tools.
   b. If upgrading the older (2012) Nexus 7 tablet, be sure to select the correct model being upgraded (i.e. 16GB, 32GB WiFi, or 32GB WiFi+GSM).

---

[8]http://www.pwnieexpress.com/wp-content/uploads/2015/05/Pwn-Pad-Community-Edition-Factory-Image-Installation-Guide.pdf

Chapter 6: Building a Tactical Hacking Tablet

Items number 7, 8, and 9 look like this:

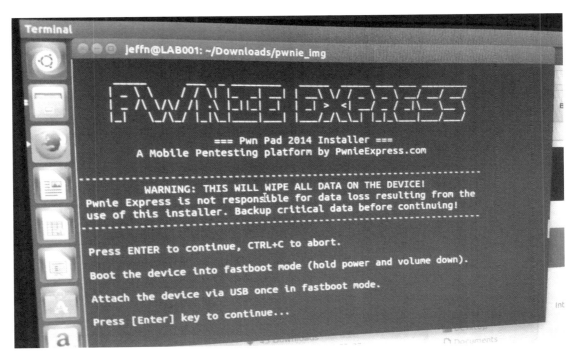

And finally it will look like this:

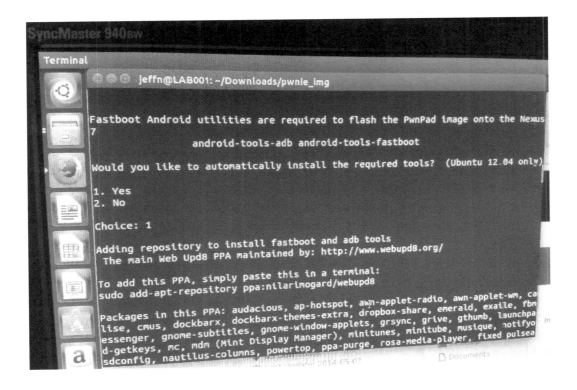

Introduction to Tactical Hacking: A Guide for Law Enforcement

The final instruction here is critical: *"Do not interrupt the process on the device"*. I can vouch for the fact that if you do, you may turn your tablet into a paperweight. This can also happen if you try to perform these steps with this software on anything other than the specific model number and make of Nexus 7 for the installation package you are using.

Use the default USB cable that came with the Nexus. That is important, but mine didn't come with the default cable in the box. I tried several I had lying around and found that an older Blackberry USB cable worked just fine, as well, so don't give up the project if you can't locate the original cable. Try a different Original Equipment from Manufacturer [OEM] USB cable if you can find one, until it works.

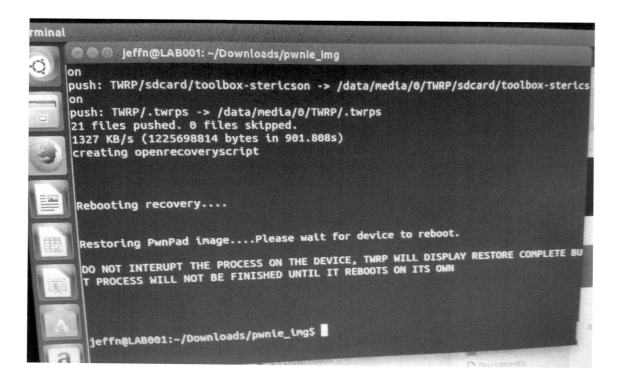

Chapter 6: Building a Tactical Hacking Tablet

When you boot the PwnPad for the first time it will look like this. You will continue to see "No Service" on your tablet until you get and activate a Cellular SIM card for your device:

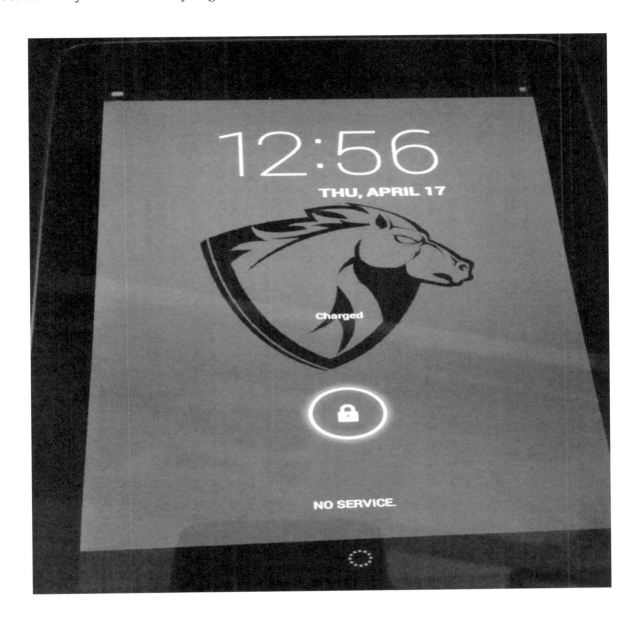

Introduction to Tactical Hacking: A Guide for Law Enforcement

With Wireless Tools:

Bluetooth Tools:

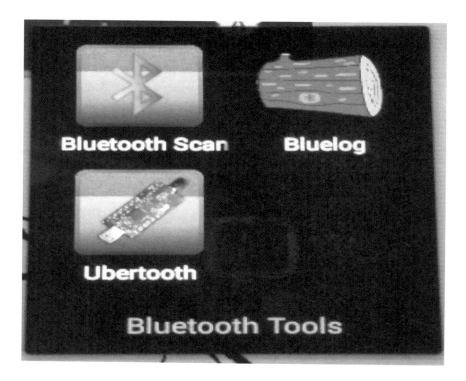

Network tools:

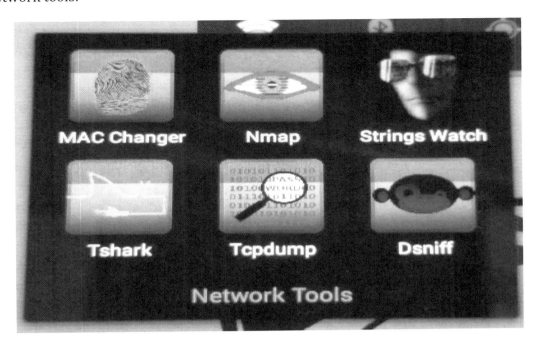

So now you have a bootable, much more portable version of the Kali Linux build, with a lot of additional features built into it, and a portable Laptop with Kali Linux you can use in a patrol vehicle, or in your lap if you had too.

With the PwnPad you can set it up for reconnaissance activity and leave it running next to your target's building or vehicle to see what is going on. Your target is not likely to notice, much less be suspicious of you carrying a tablet.

Once you connect your Bluetooth antenna and Wi-Fi adapter, you will have a truly portable Penetration Testing solution that can detect, enumerate, and potentially compromise your target's available Bluetooth, Wi-Fi, and wired computer networks. Cellular is significantly more difficult, but we'll get to that in another chapter.

Chapter 7: Tactical Hacking Wi-Fi Scanner

Now let's talk about the absolutely more portable, and infinitely more hide-able Raspberry Pi Kali build. What is a Raspberry Pi? It is an extremely small self-contained computer that can be programmed to do almost anything a regular sized computer can do, within reason.

Fortunately, Kali built a Distro [See Figure 14][9] for the Raspberry Pi, so we can remotely deploy a hacking device right into our target network, either by wired or wireless networking.

It comes packed with several interfaces including: an RJ45 jack, two USB device plugs, video and audio plugs on the right side, a digital audio plug, a High Definition Media Interface [HDMI] plug that connects to most newer computer monitors and television sets, and a 40 pin IDE hard drive interface that you can either adapt to SATA for a newer hard drive or SSD.

Figure 14

This device is perfect for a remotely deployed hacking tool, which a SWAT operator can place beside a house next to the target. An operator can also plug into a switch at the target network router location or intercept the incoming cable line and install it as a cable sniffer. The possibilities, once installed with Kali, are really limitless.

Its compact size make this a great stealthy hacking tool because it can be hidden in so many amazing ways. I recommend that you put it into something your target either wouldn't notice or recognize, such as a planter pot or a telephone company connector box.

---

[9] http://www.pcmag.com/slideshow_viewer/0,3253,l=331667&a=300225&po=3,00.asp

Chapter 7: Tactical Hacking Wi-Fi Scanner

I found an excellent tutorial on installing the Kali version for ARM processors. This is used in Raspberry Pi devices because of their energy efficiency and lower temperature operating gradient. I purchased for this kit [See Figure 15] from Amazon.com for $69.00: As you can see from the pictures, this is a very small device, and the reason I ordered the one I ordered was two-fold.

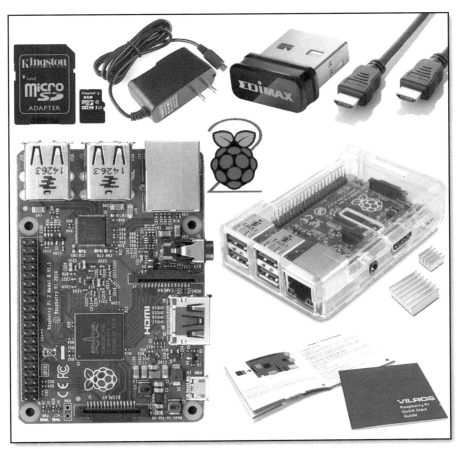

Figure 15

1. I don't have to worry about whether the Wi-Fi card, HDMI cables, power supply, case, cover, or heat sinks will work with it.
2. It has everything I need for my project, plus I can use it for other projects if I want to later.

You can purchase any kit you want, or just the bare board like in the pictures above, and the bare board will only set you back about $40.00. What do I do with it you ask? A lot of things. This device can do most of whatever you want it to, and more than you could ever dream of.

By the way, I had a 32 GB Micro SD card lying around from another project and I decided to keep the 8 GB Micro SD card pre-loaded with New Out Of Box Software [NOOBS] to play with another time. NOOBS is a project piece of software designed to help those who are new to the Raspberry Pi hardware set it up. It is created with the premise that you have a different operating system in mind than we do, and provides a point and click GUI [pronounced gooey and standing for Graphical User Interface] to help you set up the Raspberry Pi with specialty operating system builds such as: Rasbpian, Ubuntu Mate, Snappy Ubuntu Core, OSMC, Open Embedded Linux Entertainment Centre [OPENELEC], PINET [a Raspberry Pi Classroom Management Solution], and RISC OS [a non-Linux distribution].

Interestingly, the Raspberry Pi 2 is a tiny computer, with a processor and RAM. Its hard drive is the SD card, so the Raspberry Pi will attempt to boot from the SD card every time it is turned on.

Introduction to Tactical Hacking: A Guide for Law Enforcement

Therefore, we need to get the image we want the Raspberry Pi to boot into, and copy it to the SD card in a format the Raspberry Pi will recognize and be able to mount or boot from.

The tutorial tells me to download the Kali Linux ARM package from the Offensive Security download page[10] and I selected the package for the Raspberry Pi 2. The instruction page I located suggested using the Windows version of the installer, but as I described with the PwnPad, this is a bad idea, and infinitely more complicated than using the Linux build we already have because we did it with our PwnPad already, so let's use the same Ubuntu box we built for the PwnPad image and follow the instructions in the kit for the Raspberry Pi 2 build.

The author states that we can use the Disk Duplicator [DD] command in Linux. Assuming the image file from the Kali download page is named "kali-1.1.1-rpi2.img.xz" it should have recognized and installed the SD card as /dev/sdc. Navigate to the desktop download following the same instructions from our PwnPad build and type in the Terminal window: "dd if =kali-1.1.1-rpi2.img.xz of =/dev/sdc".

However, using my newly built Ubuntu box, there is a GUI version of DD called Disk Image Writer and when I right-clicked on the "kali-1.1.1-rpi2.img.xz" image I had downloaded, I was given the option to use it, so I did. Then I chose the 32 GB Micro SD card I selected earlier to use for the Raspberry Pi 2. Select "Start Restoring" after a prompt that warns the "disk image is 29 GB smaller than the target device."

Building the image on your SD card can take a while depending on your device speed, card reader speed, and image size, which, when I downloaded it was 485 megabytes. They recommend a "Type 10" SD Card, but that can be difficult to determine, so you may have to ask when you order them, or just read through the card description, or better yet, order the same kit I did, which comes with a Type 10 SD Card.

After receiving my kit, I just put the SD card I had built the Kali image on into the slot, put the heat sinks on the chips, put the Raspberry Pi into the case that came with it in the kit, inserted the Wifi USB dongle, plugged it into my nearest HDMI TV, added a keyboard, and plugged in the power supply.

The red LED came on to symbolize power received and the system immediately began booting from the SD Card. After this, you should see the Kali login screen. As with all Kali images, the user name is Root, the password toor (root backwards, super complicated) and it defaults to a command prompt after login. Don't panic, most Linux distro's can be booted into a GUI (Graphical User Interface) by starting a program, and Kali is no exception, just type startx.exe and hit enter.

You need to be able to just drop this device into a network and run your Kali tools remotely in order for this device to be of much use to you, based on how small and deployable it is, so first connect the Pi to your network, either by wired or Wi-Fi networking, then open a terminal window Look at the menu bar across the bottom of the screen and you'll see a little picture of a screen with a command prompt.

Open the terminal window and type "ifconfig" so you can figure out what your IP address for the Raspberry Pi is on your network. Once you have it written down [mine was 192.168.10.25], type nc-1-p6996 –e/bin/sh, which will open a Netcat listener on your Pi. Netcat listener is similar to a remote controller that sits open and awaits instructions to activate something. Next, start the device controller that will send signals to the remote controller. This way you can begin a Netcat session on another computer, using the same wired or wireless network as the Pi.

I'll use my Ubunto workstation and enter "nc 192.168.10.25 6996" which opens a control terminal to the Pi.

---

[10] https://www.offensive-security.com/kali-linux-vmware-arm-image-download/

Chapter 7: Tactical Hacking Wi-Fi Scanner

Wi-Fi is similar to cellular in that it sets up a "preferred network list" like that of a cellular tower list of a cell phone. The difference is that the Preferred Network List [PNL] can change anytime, as the Wi-Fi user adds a trusted Access Point [AP] by its Service Set Identfier [SSID]. The Wi-Fi device constantly sends out probe requests looking for the networks in its PNL, which may be a home network, work network, Starbucks, AT&T, or whatever trusted Wi-Fi they may have associated with their device.

Hak5 networks has created a Pineapple Wi-Fi device that is designed to receive Wi-Fi signals and copy them for a Man in the Middle attack. The Pineapple uses PineAP as a Rogue AP software program to allow you to insert yourself into a Wi-Fi network as if you were the authorized Access Point, which leads the users of the authorized AP to pass all traffic through you.

PineAP is a program within the firmware of the Pineapple that sets up rogue AP's to spoof trusted networks from the PNL. A device such as a cellular phone will connect to a trusted network, like "home" and once you've entered the password and connected to that trusted network once, it will be added to the Preferred Network List, which assigns that network trusted access.

This means that whenever your cell phone comes within range of "home" it will connect to "home" as a trusted network, and begin using "home" to get the internet instead of using the cellular network any longer.

The device may have any number of items in the Preferred Network List, and the attackers know that, so they will have a canned set of the most common PNL hosts in their broadcast list.

For example, if I want to spoof the Wi-Fi at Starbucks, I will walk into the Starbucks and run the PineAP (or just turn on the Wi-Fi scanner that comes default with my phone) and it will show available Wi-Fi networks. If I add the name of the available Wi-Fi network to the PineAP suite in the Pineapple, it will associate to the Starbucks network, hold it hostage briefly while sending "deauth" packets to all current users of the Starbucks network to get the devices already on the network off of it, then the Pineapple will send out "Hi, I'm Starbucks" and all of the devices that just got kicked off of Starbucks will see that Starbucks is back up and reconnect, with a trusted connection, and without any passwords being exchanged.

From that point forward, all traffic flowing from the devices to the internet are passing through the Pineapple first, then Starbucks out to the world, and when the responses come back, they pass back through Starbucks, then the Pineapple to the originating requestor device [See Figure 16].

See any problems with this? The owner of the Pineapple can see everything being sent and received over the Starbucks Wi-Fi by every device in the store, and all of the users think they are using their trusty Starbucks network to check their bank accounts and Facebook.

We can use this device, and others like it, to do the same thing with our target network, and observe all traffic our target is sending and receiving.

The Pineapple can even "spoof" or pretend to be the actual physical MAC address of the Starbucks router so that standard security protocol checkers won't even skip a beat. It can also select the MAC address of only ONE target device and force just that one target device through the Pineapple, leaving the others to happily share the Starbucks network. That is actually our preferred result in Tactical Hacking. We only want to be surveilling the network activity of our target, not everyone else on the Xfinity network.

When you first activate the pineapple device it drops one of the two Wi-Fi interfaces into monitor mode, which begins listening for devices beaconing for their PNL AP's, then uses the second Wi-Fi interface to beacon the rogue access points discovered by the monitoring interface.

The Pineapple can use either an ethernet jack or USB Wi-Fi device to connect to legitimate Wi-Fi signal, or a 3g or 4g modem to provide the access that gets slung back to the controller of the device.

The key to Wi-Fi, or any data decoding across a network really, is capturing "packets", opening them up for inspection, and then understanding what each piece inside the "packet" is and what it does/means.

63

Introduction to Tactical Hacking: A Guide for Law Enforcement

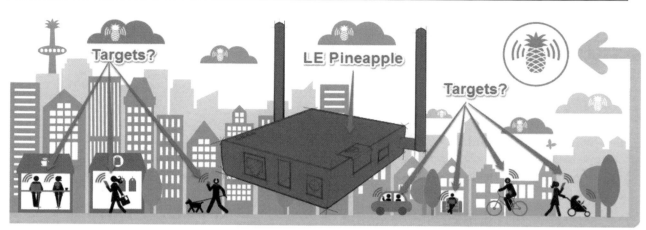

Figure 16

You've now got a full sized workstation running Ubuntu Linux and Windows 7 if you had that on there when you installed Ubuntu, a laptop running Kali Linux [and also potentially Windows 7], a Google Nexus 7 Tablet running the PwnPad version of the Kali Linux tools, a Raspberry Pi with Kali Linux running on it, and a Pineapple from Hak5. That's five super powerful Penetration Testing and Ethical Hacking tools you can use in the field, in your lab, in your car, in an armored vehicle, or just toss it in the bushes and go somewhere safe to remotely control it.

Chapter 8: Reconnaissance Tools

Several of the tools in Kali won't really apply to law enforcement because they pertain to network testing. These are geared toward network administrators and connectivity issues, as they help determine where problems within a computer network are occurring. That said, there are many other tools that will assist us in our mission, to enumerate and discover electronic communications devices nearby, and determine how they are being used, potentially even discovering what is being sent or received by the subject of your investigation.

Fern Wi-Fi cracker [See Figure 17]: This is a simple GUI frontend [shorthand for an item that runs code in the background] for Aircrack, which has been the go-to Wi-Fi hacker tool since it came out in the late 2000s. It will search the airwaves around you and tell you all of the networks it detects, even if they are "hidden." Then it will tell you the security that particular network is using and run known vulnerability cracks against it to attempt to break open the key database, allowing access to the wireless network. This could be a critical tool for you in your initial enumeration phase, where you are scanning the world around your subject to identify possible networks he could be using to communicate.

This tool is included in Kali builds and if you use it to crack your own lab Wi-Fi networks using varying degrees of complexity with your passwords, you will learn a substantial amount about Wi-Fi security in a very short period of time.

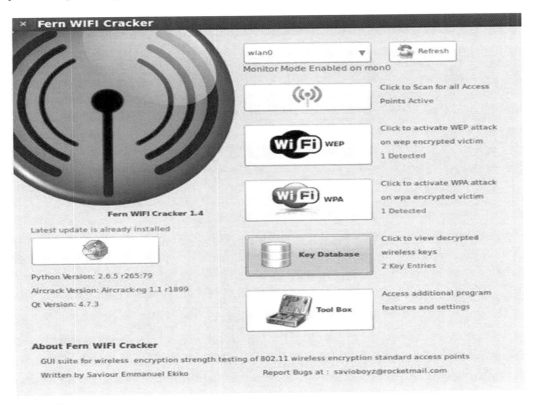

Figure 17

Introduction to Tactical Hacking: A Guide for Law Enforcement

Burpsuite: This tool performs web application security tests in an effort to initially map and analyze vulnerabilities in web pages or applications such as the target's Comcast modem, AT&T Wi-Fi box, DVR's in the subject residence, or even security camera systems with a DVR that are web enabled within your subject's building. That also includes any other web-facing or network enabled device with an application interface you could defeat to access the system, along with each and every trusted computer device in the target residence/business.

Across the top of the Burpsuite window [See Figure 18] there are a bunch of tabs, each corresponding to the types of tools you can use within Burpsuite. By clicking each tab and then running the corresponding commands, proxy, spider, scanner, sequencer, decoder, comparison, CSS (Cross Site Scripting) type code scans, passively and actively, against webfacing devices, Burpsuite can help you gain access to devices your target is using to communicate with, or to conduct anti-surveillance activity against you.

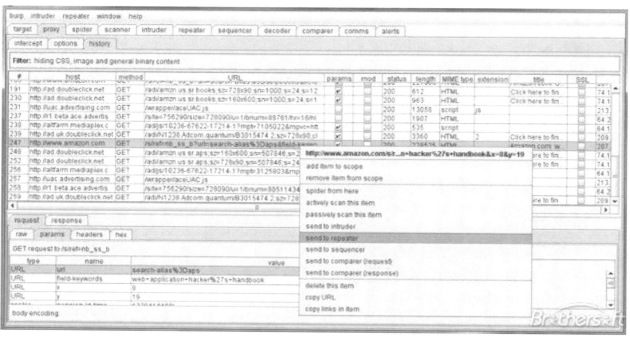

Figure 18

HYDRA brute force password cracker: HYDRA uses password lists to crack passwords. This sounds easier than it actually is, but password cracking tools like this are actually just reverse encryption or comparison engines. You may have heard that cracking a complex 14-character alphanumeric password with special characters would take, "more than 100 years to break with existing computer technology," but that assumes you are simply running through every possible password combination one at a time until you stumble across the correct one.

Modern password crackers have taken most, if not all, of the work out of password cracking by not actually unlocking the password, but by finding/matching the password. Basically, the way encryption of a password works is a series of letters, numbers, special characters and so on are selected by the user to secure their software or hardware application or device, this is called the plaintext (usually password.)

The user enters the password/plaintext into a field and the system uses complex mathematic algorithms to assign a randomly generated code that represents each letter of the password, turning it into ciphertext. This is usually the result of using a cryptographic cipher (a "cryptographic cipher" is the mathematical calculation process agreed to by an elected Standards Group to actually scramble the message. Some commonly known cryptographic ciphers used in Wi-Fi are AES, WEP, SHA, etc.) and a secret key selected by the program or the user.

There are two basic forms of encryption that are most commonly used in the world today outside of ridiculously secure military channels: symmetric and asymmetric. Symmetric encryption uses a single secret key to both encrypt and decrypt the message, data, or device. Asymmetric encryption uses a pair of keys, one public and one private.

The public key is available in a phone book for anyone to download any time they want to send you a message that is encrypted. The private key is kept by you, secured by not storing it anywhere it could be located. Without your private key, a message encrypted with your public key cannot be unencrypted. However, this does not prevent it from being found/matched. The combination of all of these randomly generated codes is then applied to the user name and stored in a database that is further encrypted a second time with another code called a "Salt" or "Hash" that further decreases the likelihood of random guessing any of the letters.

The strength of the password is dependent upon how difficult it is to figure out each character, and on the fact that the password cannot be "figured out" after only a few characters have been deciphered. You cipher a character with an encryption algorithm when you encrypt it, and you decipher the characters when you unencrypt it.

Really strong encryption is measured by the number of iterations, or times a digit is scrambled. If my password is "GOD" there are only 26 possible combinations per letter before you figure it out, right? Twenty-six letters of the alphabet times three digits, is a maximum of 78 possible combinations of letters. If you get to 'G' in only six characters, then to O in 15, and guess that go might be "GOD," then you've done my password in only 22 guesses.

But what happens when you take each of the letters and apply an encryption algorithm to it, then apply 256 iterations to each letter? Now it will take you 256 times 26 or 6,656 guesses just to get one of the 256 possible characters my first 'G' has, then another 6,656 to guess the second, and 6,656 to guess the third. I'm probably wrong on the math here, but that is a lot of calculating that would take a long time to get completed. Keep in mind that you wouldn't even know you had the right letters until you tried them in order and got access to the application requesting the password. Let's hope your "Princess Diary" app has a password lockout setting lower than 19,968 failed attempts.

So HYDRA cheats. HYDRA and the other tools like it [John the Ripper, Brutus, RainbowCrack, Wfuzz, Cain and Abel] use what's known as a Dictionary Attack, among other tools, where lists of words gathered from dictionaries, social media networks, email scanning, Twitter updates, really anywhere it can find lists of words people commonly use, and it applies the known encryption algorithms to these giant lists of words to create encrypted versions of the lists.

Instead of applying every possible character in the world to every possible encryption algorithm and forcing it into the password entry screen, it takes your encrypted password from the registry of your computer, or any of a number of other places it is stored in your system or in transit between your system and your bank, and compares your encrypted password to the giant lists of already encrypted words in its database and looks for a match. Sounds difficult, but it is actually exponentially faster than brute forcing the password character by character. This is why it is CRITICAL that you not use words in your password that are common, exist in a dictionary, or could be attributed to you. So using "password12345" may meet your password complexity requirements at your workplace, but it is unlikely to survive a password attack for long.

If you think about it, your anti-virus software does almost exactly the same thing. It takes a list of "signatures", which are compilations of known malicious software code, and compares every single little snippet of code, email, text, program, that comes across a known attack vector (Web, email, TOR, Twitter, Facebook download) anything that comes into your computer against that list until it finds a match, and yet, your computer is able to work on all of the other tasks you give it

67

Introduction to Tactical Hacking: A Guide for Law Enforcement

while the Antivirus runs all of those comparisons in the background. To be fair, most AV programs cheat by only checking code in executable files, as finding a virus in a photograph is unlikely to be as dangerous as that nifty new browser you just downloaded that is hiding it in the "install.exe" file. Yes, the AV will find the malicious code hiding in the photograph the next time it scans your system completely (something you should make it do at least once a week)_but it isn't critical because you can't "execute" a photograph.

So rather than try to crack your password mathematically, digit by digit, it just looks for a match between your already encrypted password, and giant lists of known words that have been encrypted with the same cipher already as well. Much faster, like years faster, than trying to crack your password digit by digit against all possible matches.

These programs also run frequent updates to add common words or "trending" updates to the password lists, as people will commonly use things they are hearing about in the news to help them scramble yet another password together when they come to work after a long weekend to find their password "expired again" and they have to come up with a new, unique one on the fly. I won't even discuss how many people added "HoneyBooBoo" to their password lists when she became a "trending" topic a few years back. The funny thing is, if you just tweaked it a little, "H0n3y-B0o_b00" is not really a bad password.

HYDRA has built in interfaces with a huge range of target computer services and can just connect and crack into AFP, FTP, HTTP [Hyper Text Transfer Protocol], IMAP [Internet Message Access Protocol], LDAP [Lightweight Directory Access Protocol], MySQL, Oracle, POP3, RDP [Remote Desktop Protocol] RSH [Remote SHell], SMB [Server Message Block], SMTP [Simple Mail Transfer Protocol], VNC [Virtual Network Computing], and VMware [virtualization software that allows you to run multiple computers inside one computer hardware base], to name a few.

Doesn't leave much to the imagination. Basically, if you use it in a computer today, HYDRA knows how to get and crack your password if it can connect to your system. Not good for us, but good for us when we are trying to use it on a target. Think of how many ways all those services are used today by your average internet connected device and you will realize that if you can find a way to connect to it, you will be able to get into it eventually.

John the Ripper: John the Ripper is a lot like HYDRA, but specializes more in the services, protocols, and mechanisms used by Unix-based operating systems and applications. It specializes in the more esoteric versions of Unix-based operating systems like BeOS, Open VMS, DOS, and, to an extent, Windows.

It is also more of a command line driven software program, which will drive you nuts unless you really like hammering away at the keyboard for hours trying to figure out what the MAN pages (Help menus for unix gurus) and the original programmer meant when he figured out how to word stuff. Thank goodness there is a GUI for it that automates a bunch of the command line stuff, making using this program much more user friendly. Find the GUI under Johnny, also within Kali. Password crackers, and really all of these tools, are pretty much equal in value.

Maltego: I could write an entire book on this amazing tool. It is a "Relationship Analysis Tool," but that doesn't begin to do it justice. Maltego uses the API calls for all, and I do mean all of the social media and search engines on the planet to give you the ability to search for something, then see all the connected things/people/events related to it.

Social engineering is as much an art as a function within the Intelligence Gathering arena. The Hacker Conference DEFCON has a Social Engineering contest every year where contestants have to work their way through a series of challenges live, in front of an audience, using only their best Social Engineering tools and tricks. This type of contest is a really good test of the Tactical Hacker's ability under fire because when they are at an incident, pulling it off live, people's safety and lives may be on the line.

The goal in social engineering is to gather as much information about the target as possible, while simultaneously convincing someone to take actions or give up intelligence that they would

68

Chapter 8: Reconnaissance Tools

not normally ever do, or provide. In a TH incident, social engineering may take on a much more critical role. You may find yourself having to convince the cell phone company that you are the target in order to change a password to allow you access to their account.

You may have to exploit people's natural urge to help, create sympathy, exploit trust, appeal to their curiosity, greed, and narcissism. These are the watch words of the social engineer. In a way, police officers are already social engineers, we just employ truth and common sense in a way most people aren't used to.

Usually, social engineers will send out trick emails with malware attached to try and get people to activate the file, but there won't be much call for that in a tactical hacking incident, though if it lasted as long as the Sacramento one did, you would certainly have time to try Phishing out.

Phishing is using an email specially designed to look like a legitimate email from the phone company or Ebay (or any other trusted source) to get a subject to click on an attachment that will then activate malware designed to allow you access to their machine. The best example of a very successful phishing attack was the Anna Kournikova computer virus which was a specially designed computer worm that tricked users into activating it by promising the virus link actually contained a scintillating picture of the famous and beautiful tennis player. Once the target clicked on the file the virus copied the target's email address list and replicated itself to all of the email addresses inside. The worm was very successful and infected untold millions of computers around the world in a matter of minutes.

But that leads me to a very important point. Don't launch an email that will ever go beyond your target. The email with a nasty payload has to be a drop-dead email, that can't go anywhere beyond your target computer. In fact, you really should stay away from this type of activity unless you really know what you are doing.

Sometimes social engineers will exploit the target's interests or curiosity. In a tactical hacking incident, you may find the target wishes to talk to the "press." So sending an email with a link allowing you access to his computer that purports to originate from a local news agency would be a great way to manipulate that interest. Phishing messages can also be designed to look like they are coming from the target's bank or insurance company, really anywhere that the target will not be suspicious of the origin. If you can figure out who his trusted friends are, you could craft an email from one of them, as well.

You should, at a minimum, try to gather the target's name, and any aliases, email addresses, phone numbers, titles, business relationships, significant others, hobbies, relatives, favorite foods, animals, software, hardware, even knowing their favorite adult film star could reveal a tidbit of information that helps you guess or brute force a network device password or email account password. No piece of information is too insignificant. Open source intelligence gathering tools like Maltego can plunder an amazing amount of data in a very short period of time. Using the resources identified there you can find Facebook accounts, Twitter handles, LinkedIn relationships, even comments the target may have made in response to a particular blog subject.

You can use Stack overflow with Google to identify PDF's, Word Documents, Excel Spreadsheets, and other documents that may contain metadata. Metadata can also contain GPS coordinates where a photograph was taken, usernames, software versions, and paths to the data on the target's computer, which can aid you in directed network resource mapping attempts.

For example, I put in my name and asked it to do a "basic" search. It found a phone number I had in college, the address I lived in for one month between two other addresses, a credit card number I had used once to purchase something online whose merchant database was later compromised and published to a Pastebin account. Pastebin is a type of web application for storing plain text, but is frequently used to share small bits of computer programs people want to have reviewed by their peers. Easy to read, follow, understand, and do additional research on.

Kali has the full tool built in, but it does require a fair amount of processing power, and a healthy Internet connection as it searches over 1,000 social media sites, links, and connections.

Introduction to Tactical Hacking: A Guide for Law Enforcement

There is a free and a commercial version. If you can afford it buy the commercial type for something like $800 per year, but the free version will allow you to do an amazing amount of discovery in a short amount of time, and may be all you need as long as your subject is fairly prolific.

These are all valuable tools, but how do you apply them in the field? Let's try one on for size, shall we?

SCENARIO:

Call comes out of a subject off his meds. In California we call those 5150's, which provides for certain licensed professionals to place someone on an involuntary [up to] 72-hour hold for mental health evaluation if they are determined to be a danger to themselves, danger to others, or gravely disabled as a result of a mental condition.

It is reported that the subject has locked himself in the upstairs bedroom of a house with a shotgun and the three-year-old visiting from next door.

SWAT is activated and you arrive nearby to assist with the assessment of the scene. As a tactical hacker, what could you do? Well, let's break out our trusty PwnPad and fire up a Wi-Fi assessment using Wifite [See Figure 19]:

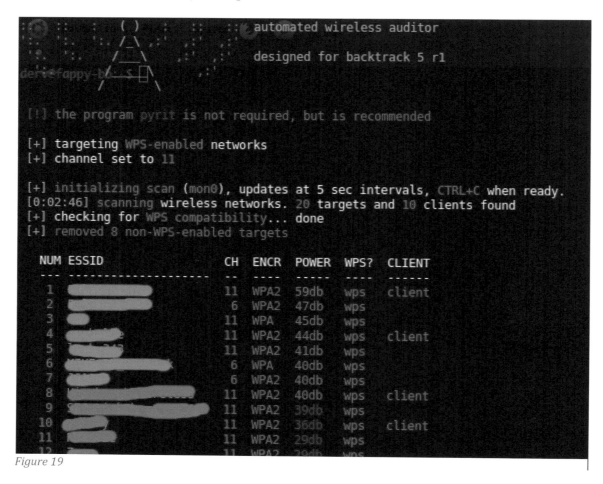

Figure 19

You are likely looking at targeting the top Wi-Fi network because it is the most powerful [look at the column labeled power], therefore the closest to you. Make sure you are right up against the target location if at all possible, and if you have the resources, have someone ask the nearby neighbors what their wireless network names are just to be sure. (They are greyed out in the photo above in case you were wondering why you couldn't see them.)

Chapter 8: Reconnaissance Tools

You can use the column entitled "Power" to determine the strongest signal. The higher the DB number the more powerful the signal, simple radio signal strength stuff. Once you've identified the potential target Wi-Fi network, you can use any of the following command lines to begin your enumeration:

to crack all WEP access points:

```
./wifite.py -all -wep
```

to crack all WPS access points with signal strength greater than (or equal to) 50dE:

```
./wifite.py -p 50 -wps
```

to attack all access points, use 'darkc0de.lst' for cracking WPA handshakes:

```
./wifite.py -all --dict /pentest/passwords/wordlists/darkc0de.lst
```

to attack all WPA access points, but do not try to crack -- any captured handshakes are saved automatically:

```
./wifite.py -all -wpa --dict none
```

to crack all WEP access points greater than 50dB in strength, giving 5 minutes for each WEP attack method, and send packets at 600 packets/sec:

```
./wifite.py --pow 50 -wept 300 -pps 600
```

to attempt to crack WEP-encrypted access point "2WIRE752" *endlessly* -- program will not stop until key is cracked or user interrrupts with ctrl+C):

```
./wifite.py -e "2WIRE752" -wept 0
```

You can also just select the line number of the target network and it will attempt to crack the key, as it did successfully in the screenshot I just provided. In the example above, I targeted networks in the bottom half of the photo above, and it cracked the PIN and WPA key found for two of the five targets in just six seconds, and the third target in 269 seconds, and you could tell it to continue attacking targets if you have determined none of these were your actual target network.

While your PwnPad continues targeting and attacking network Wi-Fi signals in the area, you could also be asking any residents who were evacuated from the barricaded subject's location for information about the networking components in the house and how they are used, operated, and secured. However, with a three-year-old hostage involved, they are likely to be too frightened and worried to recall enough to answer your questions intelligibly. Also, many people do not know or understand their own network setup well enough to be of much use to you.

Introduction to Tactical Hacking: A Guide for Law Enforcement

Open your Kali Linux laptop and use the Kismet Wireless Enumeration Tool to attempt to detect the same network [See Figure 20]:

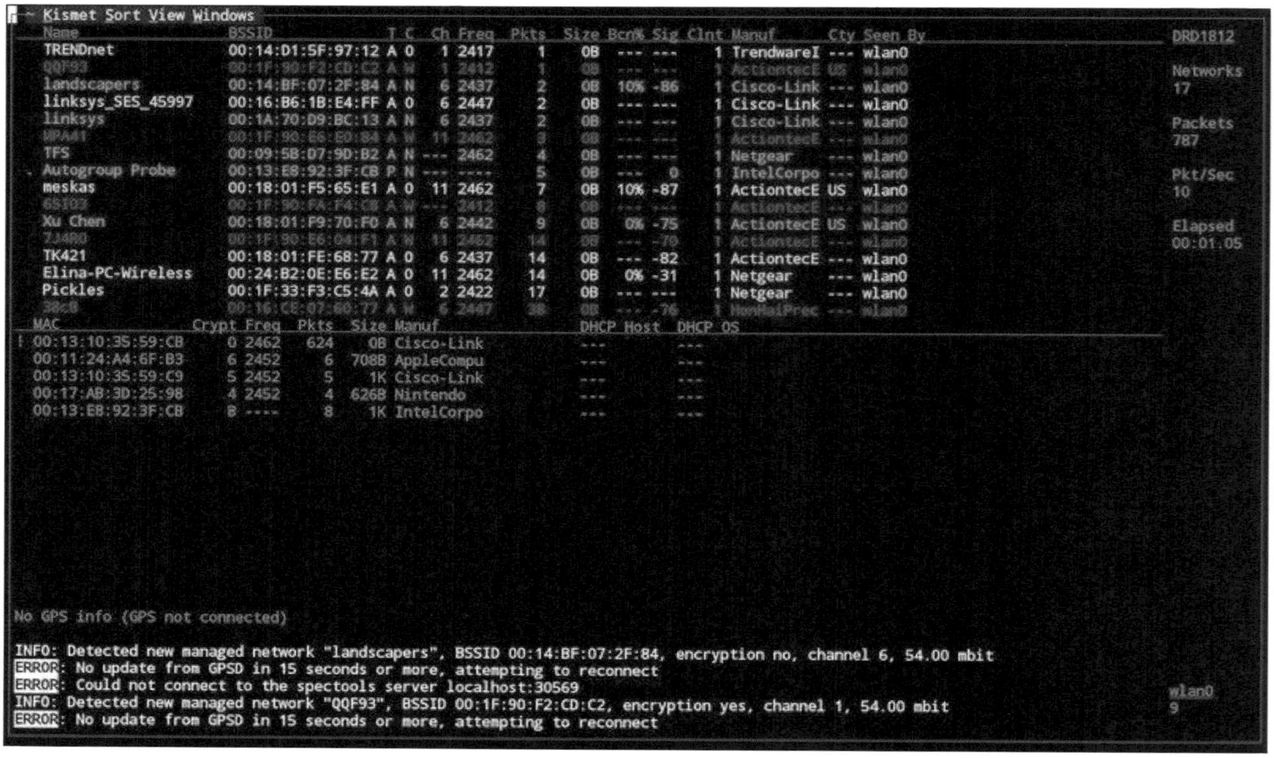

Figure 20

Notice you get a little more information here. The name/manufacturer of the network router is listed. This may be helpful to you shortly, so write it down. You should be screenshotting at this point, or you could have opened the reporting function in Kali and be taking notes and screenshots alongside your work.

On most cellular phones you can get a screenshot by pushing a combination of buttons. For instance, on my Samsung Galaxy S5 you push the down volume button and home button simultaneously. On your Google Nexus, now PwnPad, Tablet, you can click the power and volume down buttons simultaneously to get a screenshot, as well. Of course, if you need to, and you can't figure out how to do a screenshot, just take out your trusty cell phone or digital camera and take a picture of what you are seeing that you think should be included as evidence in your case.

On MS Windows machines, I like to open a Wordpad [Microsoft Word if you have it], create a blank document, and then paste all the screenshots there in order. I can go back and fill in the blanks in between with notes about what I was doing at the time I captured it later, when things have slowed down a little.

I also recommend using a voice recorder that will take and organize notes. I use Evernote because you can add photos, voice recordings, digital video and audio, and handwritten or photo scanned notes. Once you have multiple machines and apps and programs and devices running, you can lose track of who/what/when/where/why/how you did something very quickly.

Now that you've identified your target network, it's time to compromise it. Let's use Fern Wi-Fi cracker to automate some of that process. Open the program in your Kali Linux box and activate it. This will give you yet another verification of the Wi-Fi Networks you are detecting. When we get into Yagi Antennas and Cellular in my next book, I'll tell you how you can attenuate down a Wi-Fi signal until you are absolutely certain it is generating from the Target residence, but for now we'll

72

assume you are certain. Click on the antenna symbol at the top and you should see the image below [See Figure 21]:

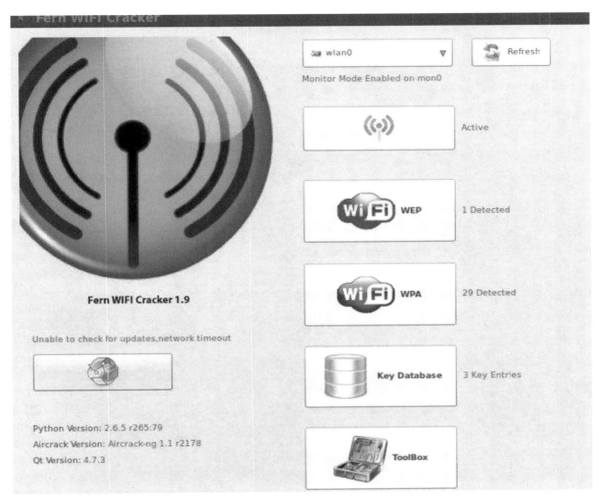

Figure 21

Notice it has detected one Wi-Fi WEP protected network, and 29 WPA Wi-Fi protected networks. Wireless Encryption Protocol is one of the first Wi-Fi encryption technologies that was published and it was almost immediately cracked and made obsolete. If we are lucky, your target network is using this. WPA is more secure than WEP, but it has also been cracked, so we are good to go defeating those networks, as well, but it might take a little longer.

We choose the network we are interested in attacking, load up a Dictionary File, or files filled with large volumes of common words, terms, and combinations that have already been encrypted by known ciphers so that they can be compared with your target's encrypted password to "match" and defeat it. Choose whether you want to do a regular or WPS attack. WPS is much faster, but you have to be much closer and not all routers have it, or have it enabled. Then just sit back and wait for the password to appear.

After you set up your lab and can run a Wi-Fi cracker without fear of accidentally accessing someone's router without permission, try your own router passwords and security to see how they fare. You'll probably upgrade quick or change the password to something super complicated.

Introduction to Tactical Hacking: A Guide for Law Enforcement

Once you've cracked the Target network's WPS or WPA key, you can access their network as a trusted user, giving you the ability to scan their network, start a Man in the Middle attack or conduct other surveillance and disruption techniques.

Go to the Fern Cookie Hijacker tool in Fern and activate it to see what the target is doing. If he opens a Facebook session, you should see the screen below [See Figure 22]:

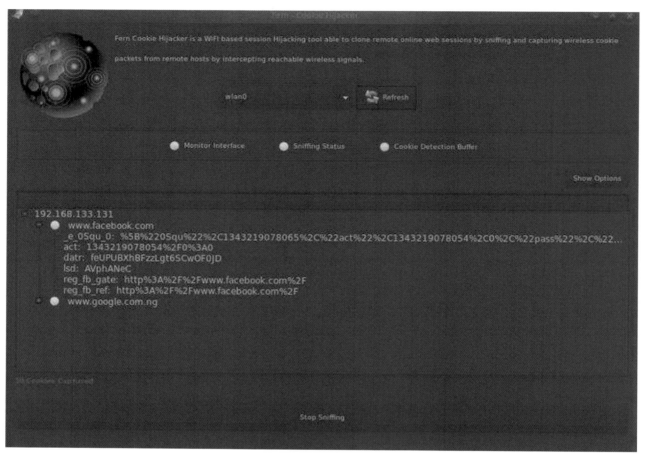

Figure 22

Which, with a little practice and timing, you can hijack, and place yourself between your target and his Facebook page, to watch all of his activity. Is the target posting pictures of the Police Officers outside and bragging he will "Take everybody with me!!" or is he frantically begging his friends for advice because he's "scared and lonely." Either way, the information will be valuable to the Hostage Negotiation Team, and you may be able to establish communication with him via this method, or take over his Facebook page and disable his access if he won't speak with you, giving you a valuable bargaining tool and forcing him to communicate with you.

What else could you hijack to intercept, surveil, compromise, or control? Email? Social Media? Basically anything with a login session can be hijacked once you establish yourself on your target's network and begin a session hijack like the one I just showed you above.

The more you practice with this, the faster and more accurate you will become with it. Keep in mind, though: This type of activity is illegal in most states/countries, and *without permission, an exigency, or a written agreement,* you could get into serious hot water legally, both criminally and civilly.

Chapter 9: Collecting Cellular Data

It will be critical for you to be able to positively identify whether or not each of the following is true:

1. Your target has cellular service or a phone or device with which he/she accesses a cellular network
2. Which cellular service provider the target is using
3. How to identify your target's specific phone and transmissions [number, IMEI, signal strength, etc.]
4. How to replicate your target's usual cellular network
5. Whether you can safely put up a fake cellular tower in the area your target currently occupies without interfering with critical infrastructure or other innocent cellular users

Well, number one can be accomplished a variety of ways, but the easiest is via a search of the usual public networks like Lexis Nexis, Accurint, and Intellisys to see if your target is already listed in one of those networks with a known cellular number. Another easy way is to contact a family member, co-worker, relative, or friend and ask. That could be really quick and easy. Of course asking your local police dispatch center to check their local records or databases for contacts with the target, target address, and vehicles registered to the target, could all provide valuable information to your investigation. Basically, the more social information you can gather the better.

Once a number is located, using the online service www.fonefinder.net or similar will provide you with the service provider the phone is registered to, though sometimes that can mean digging through a few sites to verify. However, this information will be crucial to your interception, and the most critical piece of defending your access to the cellular network is going to be having been able to properly verify you were only targeting and accessing your target's cellular communications.

Once you've located the target cell phone number or IMEI or ESN [Electronic Serial Number] via public or private databases, or just off the Cellular Company's LE exigency/help line, you can use websites listed by the FCC[11] to get information about phones and systems around the world that may help you figure out how to properly set up and capture your target's cellular phone, forcing it to use your fake cellular phone tower to make and receive calls.

The best open source example of this type of technology is the OpenBTS system, which you can find more information about here: www.OpenBTS.org. They offer a free e-book download that describes how to "get started" with their system. This site and the e-book talk in excruciating detail about how to use free/low-cost equipment, open source software, and your local cellular network.

---

[11] https://transition.fcc.gov/mb/audio/bickel/world-govt-telecom.html

Introduction to Tactical Hacking: A Guide for Law Enforcement

The way it works is fairly simple. Cellular networks are strung together in a fashion that is best described as looking like a molecular chain [See Figure 23]:

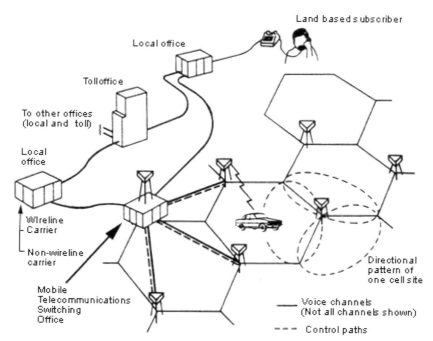

1984 Bell System Amps Plan, modified from the original

Figure 23

This allows cellular users to pass from one cellular tower to the next in what is known as a "handoff" without even knowing it, much less suffering any loss of the call or call quality. Cellular phones simply connect to the tower that provides them the most powerful signal, as that is how the phone is programmed by the manufacturer.

When you first purchase a phone from a provider like Verizon, Sprint, or T-Mobile, they will sell you cell phones that work well on their particular network and are programmed to transmit and receive almost exclusively over the radio frequencies the cellular provider has a license to operate on.

If Verizon sold you a phone that was programmed [provisioned] to work on Sprint's cellular towers and frequencies, they could be fined or have to pay Sprint directly a fee for the use of the Sprint licensed frequencies by the Verizon customer, a situation known as "roaming." This is why when you "roam" onto another cellular provider's territory, you have to pay your provider a "roaming fee," because your provider has to pay Sprint a fee to use Sprint's equipment for the Verizon customer.

What we are talking about here is inserting a fake tower near our target and fooling the target phone into thinking the tower is not only the strongest available signal for the phone to access, but is also configured for use by the cellular provider your target is a customer of. Alternatively, the fake cell tower can be used to fool other real towers in the area to provide unencrypted access to the Target's phone through use of the SS7 system protocol.

So we need to get closer to the target and provide a stronger cellular tower of the correct frequency and type (CDMA, TDMA, GSM Etc.) so that the Target phone will associate with our tower, while at the same time making certain no other phone is confused into associating with our tower. We do this by getting as close to the Target as possible, then inserting, configuring, and activating our fake cell tower [See Figure 24].

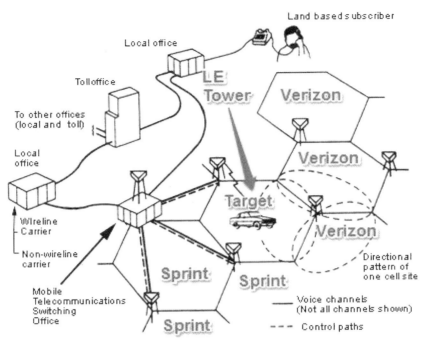

1984 Bell System Amps Plan, modified from the original

Figure 24

Our fake tower has to be able to imitate the target's cellular provider's "handshake", which is the information exchanged between the cellular device and the tower that identifies each to the other, and creates a digital agreement between them that allows them to authenticate each other and agree on protocols and services they will use to "talk" to one another, and for billing purposes.

Once the target completes the handshake and authenticates to the fake tower, they are able to place calls and send data through the tower at any time, and the target cell device will only know how to communicate with our fake tower, which has a stronger and preferable signal to the real one. After the tower is authenticated to the target's cell phone, it can now record anything from metadata to the actual call data, and can see, capture, modify, send, and falsify text, data, and phone calls. By the way, 3G simply means third generation, and 4G means fourth generation.

Why would you want to be able to do all that? There is a flaw in the SS7 system used by cellular telephone towers to communicate with each other. If you can convince two towers that you are a legitimate cell tower, they will unencrypt the data travelling between themselves, and any other cellular device connected to them. This can provide you with the ability to listen in on any caller, from anywhere in the world, seeing their text messages, hearing their conversations, live.[12]

There are situations where any of these abilities could be helpful. The important thing to remember is our goal is to safely end the standoff, and keeping outside influences from negatively impacting our ability to communicate with our target is critical to this goal. Absolute control over, or at least the ability to observe, all communications between our target and the outside world will

---

[12] . http://www.digitaltrends.com/mobile/60-minutes-smartphone-hack-ss7-flaw/

Introduction to Tactical Hacking: A Guide for Law Enforcement

be critical in safely concluding the incident. Think how damaging someone yelling "JUMP!" to the suicidal person on the bridge can be.

We need to associate the active tower with the same cellular provider so that it receives, and provides to the target, a cellular signal they can use. We do this by configuring our fake tower to replicate the target phone, a process that used to be called "Cloning" the phone, but in our case we are actually "bridging" the target cellular phone and placing ourselves in the middle of the connection. This is the "Man in the Middle" attack I've previously referred to.

A cellular phone is basically just like a police radio. It transmits on one frequency and receives on another, but the handset in a cellular device is programmed to eliminate the "Push to talk" portion you see on a Police radio, necessitating you push a button, speak into the microphone, then release the button to hear a response.

In a cellular device, once a call is initiated, the cellular device opens both the send and receive channels at the same time, sending your voice data down the send channel via the microphone, and your caller's response back on the receive channel via the speaker.

At the Blackhat security research conference in Las Vegas in 2013, I watched two security researchers use a Verizon branded Samsung Femtocell to capture, imitate, listen to, and manipulate, any cell phone within approximately 100 feet of the device, including activating the microphone before the call was initiated and listening to the target device like you would a remote microphone. They were taking advantage of the send side of the cellular phone by opening it to listen via the microphone.[13]

When you press the send button on your phone, a collection of digital data you can hear [the sounds your phone makes when you push the numbered buttons, called DTMF tones] and a collection of digital data (already imprinted on the cellular phone during the manufacturing and provisioning process) you can't hear is collected and broadcast over the send channel of the cellular device.

All cellular towers within range will see this initial sequence number and other data and respond back with an acknowledgement packet of data that the cellular device will use to identify the most powerful and appropriate tower to use to connect and complete the call, based on the type of cellular frequency, type of service available (2g, 3g, 4g, CDMA, TDMA, GSM etc.) and will send a response only to that tower, acknowledging the acknowledgement the tower sent out, and finalizing the connection, then sending the request for the call information to the tower to complete the call.

This happens in milliseconds and can be observed if you have the correct equipment and a piece of software or hardware called a "sniffer," which is capable of capturing and decoding the information in that signal in order to identify the systems being used. A "sniffer" is a device that can be used to inspect data packets in a network signal, whether over the wire, Wi-Fi, Bluetooth, or Cellular, and it is a legal device to own and use, provided you have permission to do so, such as on your own or a paid client's system.

The sniffer was originally designed to provide Network Administrators with the ability to capture raw data packets travelling through the network to inspect their contents for problematic errors that could cause, or be symptoms of, speed and reliability issues.

An example of this would be a misconfigured printer that is constantly sending out data packets on the network advertising that it is ready to receive data packets. This activity would be similar to a dog constantly barking in your neighborhood.

You already know that it's there, and the rest of the barking is just nuisance barking. This printer analogy would be an example of nuisance data. It isn't necessary for the health of the network, and it just takes up valuable bandwidth that other resources might need to use.

A sniffer can be either hardware or software in nature, with a Pineapple Wi-Fi being an example of a wireless hardware sniffer, and Wireshark being an example of a software sniffer.

---

[13] http://www.digitaltrends.com/mobile/femtocell-verizon-hack/

Chapter 9: Collecting Cellular Data

The Wi-Fi enabled Pineapple is a physical hardware device that receives the target signal, processes it, if programmed to do so, then passes it along to the original desired destination, examining all of the data packets on the network in the process.

This passive scanning activity does not harm or impact the network, and as long as the sniffer is capable of operating at the same speed as the data on the network, users will not notice any latency when the sniffer is operating.

Typically, only the cellular providers have a "sniffer" that can operate on these frequencies because the FCC has made it illegal to "wiretap" the cellular frequencies, so anyone caught doing so faces serious civil and criminal charges.

However, it is actually impossible to observe someone "sniffing" a signal out of the air because they are passively receiving the signal out of the open air, not interfering with it, just observing the signal as it flows by. A sniffer can be constructed out of common hardware parts that basically include an antenna designed for the frequencies you are in search of, hardware capable of receiving and decoding the signal, or software capable of receiving and decoding the signal. The devices that do this on the Cellular network are called "IMSI Catcher"'s, or "IMSI Sniffers."

Some of us are old enough to remember when radio scanners were popular, and when cellular phones first came out, and the service they used was not encrypted or scrambled. You could stand on a balcony with a radio scanner and listen to your neighbors' phone conversations and it wasn't even hard, or illegal at the time.

When POTS [Plain Old Telephone Service] was first offered for public use in the United States in 1878, there was one phone line installed in a neighborhood, and every house along the line had a connection. Anyone could pick up the phone and talk to anyone else (or listen in on anyone else's calls, which was much more fun) along the same line, and by pushing up and down on the receiver cradle, electrical connections were sent that would alert a telephone operator who sat in an office called a Telephone Exchange where each phone line from each neighborhood terminated.

Only the Telephone Exchange operator could generate a ring tone, and every phone on the line would ring at the same time, so everyone would pick up and the operator would announce to everyone on the line who the call was for. Now POTS lines are electronically switched to connect callers to each other, and each line terminates at a specific physical location, on the outside of your home or business, in a phone box known as the "Demarcation Point."

Hint: You can use a lineman's handset to plug into your target's phone line at the telephone pole or the Demarcation Point. The target phone is sending out a packet of data [See Figure 25] that identifies it by several important pieces of data:

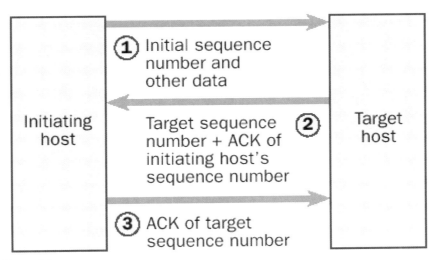

Figure 25

Introduction to Tactical Hacking: A Guide for Law Enforcement

In this diagram, which is actually a diagram of the TCP Computer Protocol exchange, the "Initiating Host" is your target's cellular phone, and it is trying to reach a cellular "Target Host" which would be the cellular provider tower for his cellular provider. If you are within range [usually under 1/8 mile without an enhanced antenna] and have an antenna and software or hardware designed to capture this type of data (IMSI Catcher), you can see the information rolling by on the screen. The trick here is to then identify your target among all of the other cellular devices sending out their initial sequence number and other data so that you can identify which provider and tower they are using. This can be difficult in a rural area, and darn near impossible in an urban area, but with practice, and the right equipment, you can filter out the noise and find just your target's initial sequence number.

After identifying which tower the targets cell phone is using, you have to create a fake cellular tower that mimics or "spoofs" the real tower, without interfering with the real tower's ability to assist other customers. This is a balancing act involving the use of a directed antenna and a low enough power transmitter that the real tower does not begin generating errors and dropping calls.

Once you have successfully isolated the target cellular phone and introduced your fake cellular antenna, as soon as the target terminates his current call, his cellular phone should detect that the tower you are using is stronger and switch its association to your tower.

Then you need to maintain that fake tower to control your targets calling ability, and to prevent your target from being able to re-associate with the real tower. You have to also establish a connection to the real tower so that your target gets the same service provider they are used to, but through your tactical hacker tower, effectively routing all of their cellular data through your fake tower, making you the "man in the middle."

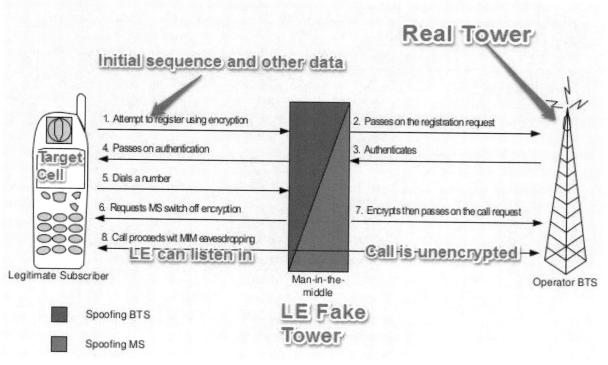

Figure 26

You must also maintain the ability to switch off the encryption most cellular phones request in their connection to the real tower so that you can listen in on the calls your target is making. This will be crucial in determining the state of mind of your target. Again, is he afraid and asking Mom what to do, or is he telling his brother he wants him to have all his "stuff" because he has set a bomb and intends to kill as many Cops as possible when SWAT rushes in to rescue his hostages?

As shown in the diagram above [See Figure 26], the data encryption normally occurs automatically after the Target cell initially contacts the Real Tower and requests to register for Cellular Service. With our Tactical Hacker Tower in between the Real Tower and the Target cell phone, the Target cell phone request to establish an encrypted connection with the tower gets denied, as the Tactical Hacker tower tells the requesting Target Cell, "I don't have that capability, so let's work together without encryption."

The Target cellular phone is usually programmed by the Cellular phone provider to accept this request if made because to insist on an encrypted connection with a tower that is broadcasting an inability to do so would result only in a dropped call, which the Cellular phone provider cannot allow very often or its customers will cry foul and switch providers. So the target cellular phone requests encryption from the tactical hacker fake tower and our tower responds, 'I'm unable to provide you with encryption but I can still handle your request for a phone call." The tactical hacker tower then passes on the registration request from the Target Cell Phone to the real tower complete with the encryption request that came from the original target cell.

The real tower responds back with an authentication code for the encrypted connection between the target cell phone and the real tower, which the tactical hacker tower then intercepts and establishes an encrypted connection between the tactical hacker tower and the real tower, but it strips out the encryption request and passes on the authentication from the real tower to the target cell phone and the target cell phone continues with the unencrypted authentication allowing it to dial a number using the tactical hacker tower in the middle.

Because the requests sent from then on through the Tactical Hacker Tower are unencrypted, the Tactical Hacker Tower can now control, monitor, intercept, and record all incoming and outgoing calls to the Target cellular phone. Using the flaw in SS7 provides the same abilities, but is a much more carefully guarded access point. Your local Cell Phone Provider can grant you access to it, but good luck having them just leave the equipment and password with you all the time.

The Real Tower is unaware its security protocols have been bypassed because the authentication between the TH Tower and the Real Tower is spoofed to fool the Real Tower into thinking the TH Tower is the Target Cell phone, which has permission to authenticate and use the Real Tower.

Watching cellular data pass back and forth to determine what the target is browsing on the internet on their cell phone is another story altogether, but can be done. It's actually easier to "spoof" a trusted Wi-Fi connection and fool the cell phone into connecting to that so that you can use Wireshark to capture and observe the network traffic than it is to capture cellular data, but that is covered in another chapter.

A smaller device that could be remotely deployed near your target in order to create this "Man in the Middle" attack is a Femtocell, but their configuration and manipulation can be exceedingly complicated unless you know a "phreak" (phone geek/hacker) who can tell you things you aren't supposed to know about ALL of the different types of telephone networks.

The phreak is sometimes in possession of illegal information that they will provide to you. Consider them similar to a Confidential Informant and work with them according to your local policies and procedures regarding CI's. Keep in mind also that phreaks do not typically want you to know what they know, as you may pass on the fact that they know something to the Telco, who then will likely lock the Phreak out of whatever privileged access they may have gained with their illicit knowledge.

Introduction to Tactical Hacking: A Guide for Law Enforcement

The better known Pineapple device from Hak5 networks can be used for MITM attacks on Wi-Fi, see the next chapter for that, but the MITM attack on Cellular networks can also be accomplished with a fairly inexpensive device [See Figure 27].

Figure 27

This device is what is known as a "Software Controlled Radio" device, and with the proper software, will allow you to transmit or receive any radio signals from 10 Mhz to 6 Ghz, which is pretty much every radio frequency currently in use, including all of the restricted and "illegal to monitor" cellular frequencies.

Software Controlled Radio uses open source hardware and software and will allow you to set up a MITM attack on pretty much any frequency if you know what you are doing. Thankfully, the website selling it offers all sorts of fantastic tutorials for the "amateur radio enthusiast", while at the same time advertising that they provide "Pineapple University tutorial videos and documentation" but primarily for "Penetration Testers." If you have the time and the inclination, and $328, this will do everything we are talking about in this chapter, and more.

Let's talk about the capabilities of live monitoring multiple social media streams via Geostreaming, where every device on the planet that attaches to a network has data flowing to it and from it. Geostreaming is "exploiting user–generated geospatial content streams."[14]

Every individual using a web connected device has a content "stream" constantly flowing from their device to the web and back. Facebook posts, Twitter posts, YouTube Posts, all the means by which the connected everyday person networks, communicates, broadcasts, and exchanges all of the everyday minutia of our daily lives via social media.

But how do we "exploit" that? First we have to "shim the stack" again, but in a way that intercepts all social media and data streams coming from a defined geographical location, so we can

---

[14] http://geocontentstream.eu/geostream/

see "hotspots" of activity in a defined area by collecting crowdsourced geospatial data from the original web sources, like Facebook, Twitter, and YouTube.

Since everybody selects "accept" when they see the End User License Agreement from Facebook and the others, they have already signed away their rights to pretty much everything on Social Networks. Companies are hard at work aggregating it into human readable form, and mapping it based on the geolocation data inserted into the header of the data packet. As a result, we turn this:

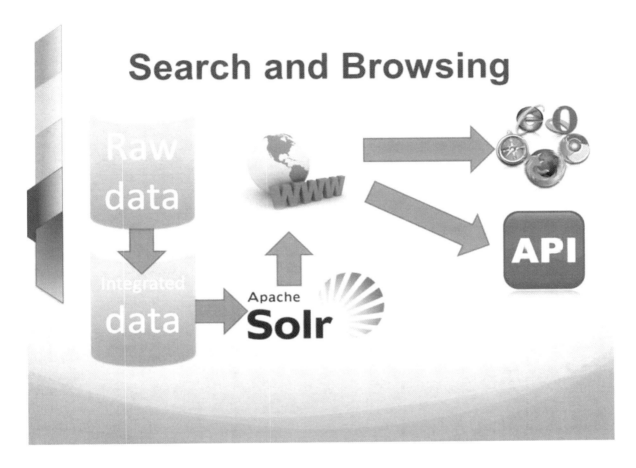

[15]

---

[15] http://geocontentstream.eu/geostream/

Introduction to Tactical Hacking: A Guide for Law Enforcement

Into this, which can tell us the exact geographical location of the victims, suspects, witness, and reluctant participants in real time.[16]

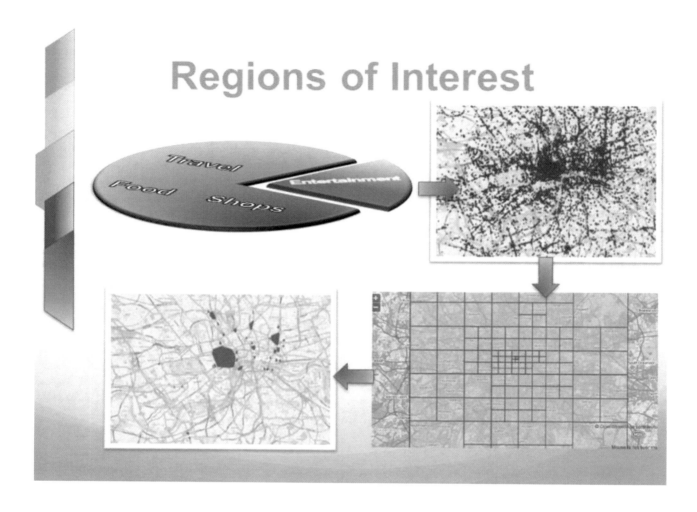

Companies like Geofeedia will provide you a point and click interface that turns the above data into something much more palatable.[17] This not only tells you what type of social media is being used by the broadcaster, but exactly where they are, what they are saying, where they are moving, and what the other people around them are saying at exactly the same time, in real-time. Of course, this comes with a hefty price, but they are taking unmanageable data streams and aggregating them into "pretty pictures." X1 has a similar product that is much more affordable, but does pretty much the same thing, just in a different format [See Figure 28].[18]

---

[16] http://geocontentstream.eu/geostream/
[17] https://geofeedia.com/products/how-it-works/
[18] http://www.x1.com/products/x1_social_discovery/#view

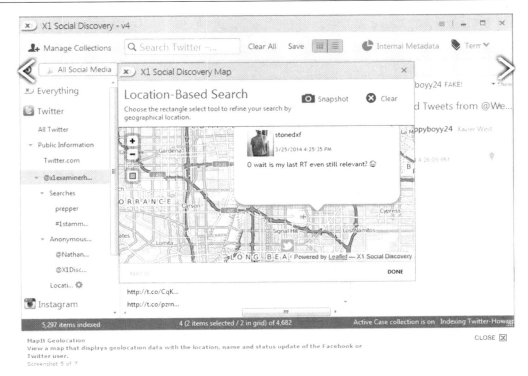

Figure 28

While you are watching to see what network transmissions from your target network are occurring, this type of streaming data media capture can show you even more of your target's accounts, that you may not have even been aware of, in real time, along with images, texts, videos, etc. from all the nearby witnesses, friends, neighbors, cohorts, and even other suspects you may not have even been aware were there, or who have potentially been helping or directing your target.

Geostreaming is in its infancy, relatively speaking, and it only works with subjects who do not have their privacy settings turned on. If your target has a VPN [Virtual Private Network], is using encryption, or several other sneaky type tools that can defeat this crowdsourced data stream, this product type will not assist you at all.

This is just another tool to add to your toolbox, and it requires a fair amount of monitoring and attention to even identify your target among many of the other extraneous posts from nearby friends, relatives, neighbors, victims, and suspects, particularly in very rapidly evolving large incidents, like the Boston, Paris or Belgium Bombings.

Chapter 10: The Best Policies, Procedures and Practices

Most of this next chapter will be very dry. Policies, procedures, and best practices usually are, but you need to become at least familiar with them, and you really should become a subject matter expert if you are going to integrate Tactical Hacking into your agency's response matrix.

As you get better at using these tools and techniques, you will find yourself engaged in digital evidence identification, collection, and preservation both in the field and the lab. The United States Department of Justice National Institute of Justice published a special report entitled, "Electronic Crime Scene Investigation: A guide for First Responders, Second Edition" in April of 2008, but I was pleasantly surprised at how detailed and accurate it was, even with the changes that have occurred in the computing field in the 7 years since it was published. Most of the items I will cover in this chapter will refer to their expert guidance in that document.[19]

It goes without saying that nothing can be safely accomplished until scene safety is established, but that doesn't mean you can't be collecting, securing, and transporting digital evidence without changing it, right from the beginning. The NIJ states the following dire consequences may occur if you don't follow Best Practices, the Law, and Privacy Acts:

"First responders must use caution when they seize electronic devices. Improperly accessing data stored on electronic devices may violate Federal laws, including the Electronic Communications Privacy Act of 1986 and the Privacy Protection Act of 1980. First responders may need to obtain additional legal authority before they proceed. They should consult the prosecuting attorney for the appropriate jurisdiction vii to ensure that they have proper legal authority to seize the digital evidence at the scene. In addition to the legal ramifications of improperly accessing data that is stored on a computer, first responders must understand that computer data and other digital evidence are fragile. Only properly trained personnel should attempt to examine and analyze digital evidence." [20]

Policies related to the collection of Live Digital Evidence need to address all aspects of the collection process, and should be based on the order of collection, which is necessarily based on the likelihood of degradation of the evidence over time. Obviously the evidence most likely to be lost needs to be collected first, so your policy should contain processes and procedures for collecting "live" data, or that which occupies volatile memory spaces, like RAM.

Volatile memory is any chip or media which will become blank or dump its contents due to loss of power or introduction of specific keystrokes or other sequences [booby-trapping]. This type of memory is usually contained in the CPU, Cache, RAM, and other electrically charged chips inside computers, tablets, phones, and other devices, and consists of the tables contained in routers and switches in network routing devices, such as the ARP cache, process table, kernel statistics, or any other temporary file system, swap space, slack space, or unallocated areas of any type of electrically charged media.

Data on hard disks and archival media are not usually volatile, however, if during your investigation you determine the Target has set booby-traps that will reach out to remote locations and wipe, delete, overwrite, or replace volatile data critical to your investigation, it behooves you to have a policy in place to deal with that remote location, whether by having an MOU in place with off-site storage management solutions hosted in the cloud, or by having emergency preservation

---

[19] https://www.ncjrs.gov/pdffiles1/nij/219941.pdf
[20] https://www.ncjrs.gov/pdffiles1/nij/219941.pdf

Chapter 10: The Best Policies, Procedures and Practices

orders pre-configured with common vendor subpoena delivery information so that you can deliver an emergency preservation order at 0200 hours anywhere in the world, though you are unlikely to need to be able to do that, for now.

Remotely hosted data that is stored in the "cloud" can create some real problems when it comes to preserving and collecting it as well. Not every country complies with US preservation orders, and you sometimes have to get creative with the parties on the other end of the phone line when contacting a Data Center in a foreign country.

For instance, I once contacted a Canadian Cellular Phone provider to request subscriber information for a phone they were hosting that was engaged in a scam. The phone provider told me they "don't honor" US subpoena's or search warrants, but "there's nothing that says I can't give you the information anyway" and he just read me all of his client's personally identifiable information right over the phone without ever even trying to validate my identity or purpose. I wasn't expecting that, but I don't think the suspect was either. I wasn't able to get the suspect prosecuted in that case, but if I had, how do you think I could/would have been able to get that statement from the phone company representative in that foreign country's statement into evidence?

The most important thing your policy and procedures should address is that the procedures used to collect the evidence should never change the evidence. But, we all know that isn't always possible, so make certain that you have procedures in place that record your actions, whether by notating what you are doing, photographing or video recording it, or using a screen grabber to image the items you are viewing/working with, or even using a live viewing capture utility like Snagit. If you have to. If you are forced to accidentally modify the data in some fashion, be able to articulate why and how you changed it, so you can testify to the change you made later, and whether that change would have critically modified the data, or even damaged it.

A perfect example of this is the "bull in a china shop" scenario, where someone in the crime scene trips and unplugs the computer with the kiddie porn on the screen, causing power to discharge, erasing everything from RAM, and making the whole computer password protected on reboot.

You can get around that loss, but you need to articulate that it was simple human error, that it didn't introduce any incriminating evidence into the target computer, and that you used "best practice" next steps to collect any evidence you recovered after that accident occurred. I recommend the following procedures for any evidence scene, but particularly for computer crime scenes:

Start by photographing everything in place, as you found it, particularly the cabling connecting devices to terminals [computers], then establish which devices are already powered on, and try not to turn them off. If you find a computer already powered off, watch the power light on the case for a few minutes to see if it slowly blinks or fades on or off, any indication that it may only be "hibernating" rather than completely powered off. If so, try to document that condition, because if you move the mouse or push a key on the keyboard the computer may restore to a powered on condition, but you did that, so you need to document that the device powered on as a result of something you did, and that you found it powered on, just in a "waiting" state.

If the screen is on and powered up, photograph it. If not, photograph that. Photograph everything, from multiple angles, with a flash and without, because you won't get the chance to do so again later. Collect live data first, it is most volatile, and if the suspect is off-site somewhere, he/she may remotely wipe any device connected to the web if he can figure out you are at his lair. Use a Wi-Fi and Bluetooth scanner from one of your Kali devices to attempt to locate any wireless devices that may be hidden in an attic, crawlspace, outdoor shed, kitchen cupboard, anywhere you could hide a Raspberry Pi [something the size of a cigarette pack] could contain terabytes of information germane to your investigation.

Try to map out your network devices to determine whether any of them contain storage. Even a newer HP printer contains memory that can have images stored within. For instance, if your

Introduction to Tactical Hacking: A Guide for Law Enforcement

target scanned checks belonging to a victim, that scan may remain in memory on the printer. Use the menu functions on the printer to look for a "history" or report function to try and establish what/how the printer was used.

Document every device you locate, where it was in the room, and what it was connected to, and how. It is nice to know there were four external hard drives in the room, but when he claims later two belonged to his roommate, it becomes much more important to know which was connected to which device when you found it, particularly if your target is the only one with the password to the device with all the goodies on it.

Look for cables leading out of the room, particularly into crawl spaces or attic or basement locations. Follow them to verify what is attached to the other end.

Document the serial numbers of every device you find, and if you are going to seize it, document that you seized the item by serial number, so later, when the four of you have had a good night's sleep and are arguing over who gets "the paper" you will each already have a list of who grabbed what and needs to document the condition it was in when they found it.

Your exigency has expired if you have time to wander around photographing things without dodging bullets or shrapnel, so you should have a search warrant by now. Relax and work in a methodical manner, either in a grid formation, or clock formation, so you work your way from one end of the room to the other, missing nothing in between, above, or below the target machines.

When you first look at a live machine, document the drive mappings (C:, D:, F:, G:) listed, particularly if they show more hard drives than you see inside the case. Look for evidence of offsite storage locations like subscription services like Dropbox. Look for programs like Viivo, as they provide encrypted offsite storage within a Dropbox, OneDrive or other cloud account, but if they don't have it set to lock automatically, this will be the only chance you get to access it without them giving you a password.

Look for links to other computers, devices, or links to networked devices. Check to see if Airdroid or other remote cellular connections are installed. Check the router in the home for USB ports, as many modern routers have USB ports allowing for external hard disks to be attached and shared across the network, and they can be housed in hidden areas around the house [See Figure 29]:

Figure 29

Also look for other networked devices, like Xbox or Playstation, Tivo, or any other DVR type device connected over the network, because computer savvy Targets can store data anywhere, including on their neighbor's unsecured Wi-Fi network, or even on a Raspberry Pi out in the garage or shed connected to an external hard disk or array. Look for directional antennas attached to the house. The longest recorded Wi-Fi connection occurred over 75 miles, so they could easily have a Wi-Fi connection established with a nearby storage unit, house, friend, neighbor, relative, anywhere with power and access to the same network.

Look for additional networks they may have connections to by running IFCONFIG on Linux computers or IPCONFIG on Windows computers. They could be running NAT rules to allow one network connection by wire to a network in 192.168.10.1 subnet, and a second network connection

Chapter 10: The Best Policies, Procedures and Practices

by wireless to a network in the 10.10.12.1 subnet, where neither can see the other, but both are accessible to his primary machine. Also look for this:

Your target may be using VMWare or Oracle Virtual Box to run computers within his computers, or "Virtual Machines." These computers are not on unless they are activated, and when they are deactivated, if they are configured correctly, they revert back to the original image, deleting all traces of everything they were doing when they were originally connected to the Internet.

This means that if your target is hosting an illegal website with kiddie porn on it, and let's face it, a lot of them do, then as soon as you power down that computer, the website will disconnect, and if configured correctly, all data stored after the original image was created will be lost. He won't care that they have to rebuild the entire thing, he will just be happy you have lost everything they were hosting.

You must also look for encryption. Encryption is our enemy when we discover it on Target computers. If it is active already and they don't give you the password, you are highly unlikely to ever be able to access it.. Viivo is a very strongly encrypted partition hosted within offsite cloud storage that scrambles when you power the machine down, but if you have the computer open and running, you may be able to simply right click and choose unencrypt, or, if you are lucky, just double-click to open it and see the contents while it is still open and unencrypted. Once power is removed from that device, the data is encrypted and safe at rest, and completely out of your reach.

Introduction to Tactical Hacking: A Guide for Law Enforcement

If hard disk encryption is detected, either visibly or by use of a logical tool like Zero-view, PGP Disk, or some other soft or hardware based encryption detection technique, have a policy in place to allow for collecting a "live" image, or a logical image of the drive, and be aware enough of the procedures in place for doing so that you could explain it later in your report. Tools like the Linux based dd.exe, Helix, or remote via vendor tools like F-Response, can allow you to image a drive while it's running, and this can be very helpful when dealing with raid setups as well, as deconstructing and reconstructing a raided server is no joke, and not for the uninitiated. Keep this problem in mind when writing the search warrant. You may need to maintain controlled access to the Suspect's residence for several days to properly image encrypted data on-site in order to preserve it in its unencrypted state.

Working with live data should be an absolute last resort, however, as any change or action taken is permanent and immediate. Once you are certain you have identified all of the connections and connected devices, cables, wired and wireless connections etc., be prepared to pull the power cord out of the back of the computer in order to transport the system to a lab.

If the computer is a laptop, or has a battery backup, try not to power it down completely until you can get it to a lab for further live examination if you have that option available. If you are powering it down on purpose, pull out the battery as well, otherwise the system will continue running. This may be fine, or it may cause you to be surveilled by your target, just depends on what software they are running on the laptop.

Diagram and label every single cord and cable, even if it isn't connected to anything, because it might have been. Sometimes the absence of a device that looks like it used to be there, or should be there, is as much evidence as finding the device itself. Document all serial numbers and the make and model of every device you come across in the house, even if you aren't taking it with you. Again, the absence of something may be just as important as the existence of that same thing, particularly if your target was barricaded for a long period of time and might have had time to hide, destroy, disguise, or otherwise conceal a small object. Keep in mind, even something as small as a thumb drive can hold hundreds of gigabytes of data these days, and is extremely easy to conceal.

Other potential sources of digital evidence can be found in and around computer devices and you may not immediately recognize them as potential evidence stores. Look for reference material like computer books and magazines that may lead you to a Target's storage cache of digital evidence.

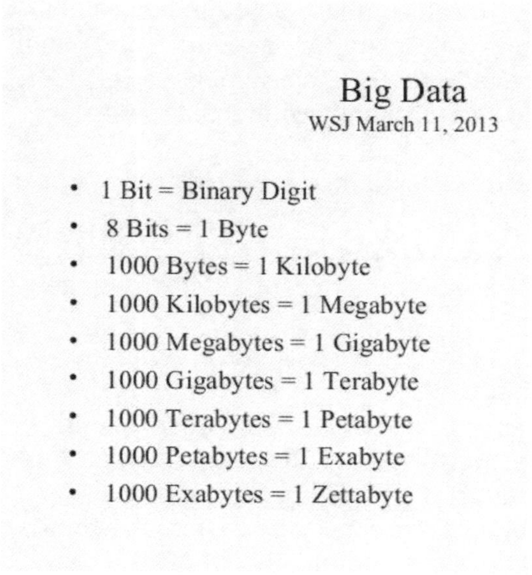

Big Data
WSJ March 11, 2013

- 1 Bit = Binary Digit
- 8 Bits = 1 Byte
- 1000 Bytes = 1 Kilobyte
- 1000 Kilobytes = 1 Megabyte
- 1000 Megabytes = 1 Gigabyte
- 1000 Gigabytes = 1 Terabyte
- 1000 Terabytes = 1 Petabyte
- 1000 Petabytes = 1 Exabyte
- 1000 Exabytes = 1 Zettabyte

Figure 30

So if one gigabyte [See Figure 30] will hold a pickup truck filled with printed paper's worth of documentation, and a thumbdrive you could hide in your nostril will hold 128 of those……you really need to be searching for anything that could hold a cockroach, which may mean tearing up carpet, looking in couch cushions and chair frames, under tables, even "packed in their suitcase" in Corrections parlance, and if you need me to explain that one, I guess the best way to put it would be to check "where the sun don't shine."

Remember also that digital evidence may also be stored on media that contains physical evidence, like fingerprints, DNA, or bodily fluids (you Corrections guys/gals can explain all the nifty ways your "clients" have discovered to "store" things) so be careful to use gloves and not damage the integrity of possible physical evidence while you are busy collecting digital evidence.

Chapter 10: The Best Policies, Procedures and Practices

Also keep in mind that processing digital evidence is complicated. It requires specialized tools, training, and years of experience to keep from seriously mucking things up, so don't touch a mouse or keyboard that might be attached to evidence unless you are the one trained and authorized by your Department to do the touching, collecting, and analyzing.

You are also inherently better off involving those more experienced, or with a specialized skill in the writing of Search Warrants pertaining to the particular materials being sought.

They may have a much better understanding of what you are looking for even if they don't know what it is. How's that you say? How can they have a better understanding of what I'm looking for even if they don't know what it is? Well, for example, if you tell an experienced computer person that you are looking for anything that could hold thousands of photographs, they don't need to know the photos are of kiddie porn, or the neighbor's juvenile babysitter sunbathing, to know that certain types of digital media are more likely to be used to store digital photo's (like memory cards inserted in a digital camera or cell phone) and they may point to an external hard disk attached to a router hidden in a crevice in the closet when all you saw was a black box with blue flashing lights on it.

Look for words like, "delete, format, remove, copy, move, cut, wipe" or on Linux devices, "rm, rmdir, cp, mv, del, deluser, delgroup." Look for open communication windows that your target may have been using to send and receive files with, and watch for active programs that allow for remote monitoring of the camera and microphone, particularly in laptops, as you may be being observed by a foe while you work.

Also look to see if there are active remote communications programs running that might allow a remote user to continue deleting or damaging files remotely even though your Target is no longer there. If you detect remote access issues, don't panic, just calmly look for ways to disconnect the computer from the network before the remote user realizes what you are doing. It is possible, just to scare you further, to set a computer to self-destruct if it is removed from the network connection it has been programmed to watch for. So keep in the mind the level of sophistication of your Target while you are searching the scene.

Have a procedure or policy in place that addresses whether you are allowed to impersonate your Target in order to keep open communications going with potential other Targets he/she may have been collaborating with. Sometimes taking over a communication "chat" with an offsite target will provide you with additional Targets. Instant Messaging windows like Skype are easy to see, but background messaging apps may be more difficult to detect. Try "Alt-Tab" on Windows computers to see all the different command windows that are open, and Terminal in Linux.

Introduction to Tactical Hacking: A Guide for Law Enforcement

More excellent advice concerning the Preliminary Interview process from the NIJ:[21]

Preliminary Interviews

First responders should separate and identify all adult persons of interest at the crime scene and record their location at the time of entry onto the scene.

 No one should be allowed access to any computer or electronic device.

Within the parameters of the agency's policies and applicable Federal, State, and local laws, first responders should obtain as much information from these individuals as possible, including:

- Names of all users of the computers and devices.
- All computer and Internet user information.
- All login names and user account names.
- Purpose and uses of computers and devices.
- All passwords.
- Any automated applications in use.
- Type of Internet access.
- Any offsite storage.
- Internet service provider.
- Installed software documentation.
- All e-mail accounts.
- Security provisions in use.
- Web mail account information.
- Data access restrictions in place.
- All instant message screen names.
- All destructive devices or software in use.

If you see anything else you don't recognize, look it up. Don't just disconnect something until you fully comprehend exactly what you are looking at/facing as doing so could potentially destroy or damage evidence or equipment.

---

[21] https://www.ncjrs.gov/pdffiles1/nij/219941.pdf

Chapter 10: The Best Policies, Procedures and Practices

Here is a flowchart from the NIJ suggesting how to Collect Digital Evidence from the Scene:[22]

Collecting Digital Evidence Flow Chart

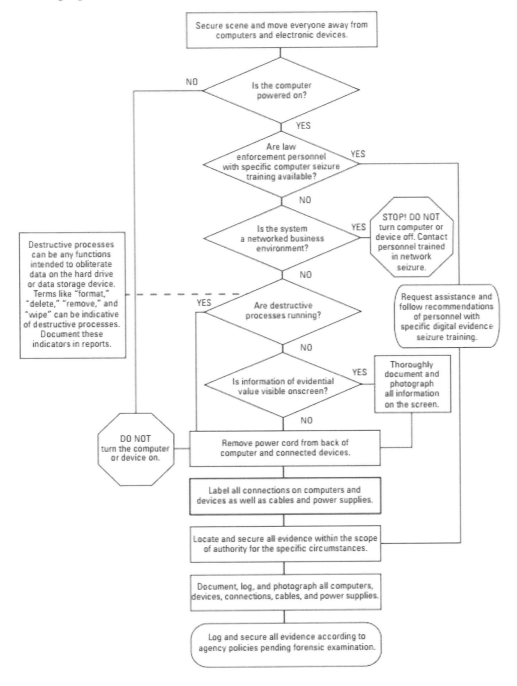

Now for the good stuff, Viruses, malware, spyware, and booby-traps. A common defense being offered in court across our great land is that the Target, "didn't do it, my computer was infected with a Virus!!" Make note of any anti-virus software running on the Target machine, particularly the version number, and try to verify whether it is actively running, and if so, what functions have been enabled/activated.

---

[22] https://www.ncjrs.gov/pdffiles1/nij/219941.pdf

Introduction to Tactical Hacking: A Guide for Law Enforcement

Windows has various tools that will accomplish this for you, but I recommend you run Metasploit and the PSExec tool to create an image of the live RAM on the machine to defeat this assertion. That is an advanced subject however, and not covered in this book.

A critical piece of the computer crime puzzle that absolutely MUST be understood and talked about in order to assure it never happens again, is the Steve Jackson Games vs. The US Secret Service case from 1990.

I'm sure that you, like me, have been told many times by your supervisors and peers that, "you never want to be the guy whose name appears on a precedent setting case." Usually this means you have either exceeded your authority, or crossed a thin line that hasn't been litigated yet, but either way, you never want to be the reason a new policy or case law is created, it just never ends well for you.

In the Steve Jackson Games case, the game company was in the business of creating fantasy board games, and was on the bleeding edge of the burgeoning computer role-playing game industry so they loosely associated themselves with the up and coming computer geniuses occupying what was the first version of the World Wide Web, Bulletin Board Systems.

BBS's were computer servers that stored digital conversation sites where people could chat about all types of subjects. Of course the first people to use and embrace this technology were the nerds who were building and creating it in their garages, sometimes literally as they were using it.

Guys, sorry ladies, but it was almost exclusively guys in the geek arena at that time, would build a computer out of spare parts, add a Modem (MOdulator/DEModulator) which was a computer card that could send and receive digital data over a standard phone line, and could connect to any other computer with a Modem that was turned on and waiting to receive calls.

BBS's were built by individuals with a knack for computers and some who wanted to run businesses that allowed people to gather on a BBS and "chat" back and forth. This "chat"ting occurred via text based messages that appeared on the screen, and it was frequently anonymous, and even more frequently irreverent of the Federal Government because the geeks were on the outside fringes of all things political, and had a general dislike/distrust of Government, who earned it, as you will see from the facts of the case.

One of the users who was using the Steve Jackson games hosted "Illuminati" BBS (each BBS had a title, users, storage space, and allowed users to upload text files of limited size to share, sort of like Facebook but without the preening and photos) was considered by the US Government to be a little too radical, and they decided that his use of the Illuminati BBS was likely insurgent and possibly even domestically terroristic in nature. He had really strong political views.

Also, the Illuminati BBS had been reposting and hosting the Phrack newsletter, which at the time was frequently publishing a printed version of articles that described how to defeat pay telephone systems by using toy whistles from the Captain Crunch cereal box to replicate the sound of a quarter being dropped into a pay phone, thereby allowing those with a penchant for knowledge, technology, and "free" long distance telephone calls to fool the pay phone into placing the calls by playing these tones into the microphone.

This type of mischief was considered theft, and it technically was, so the Telco's would frequently harass the Secret Service and other TLA's about how they were "losing millions" to teenage boys with whistles. To be fair, there were some Phreakers (telephone hackers) who were actively exploiting telephone systems for far more than quarter tones, but regardless, the losses were miniscule compared to the credit card fraud and scams we see on the internet today.

So Steve Jackson decided to work with Loyd Blankenship on a book called Gurps Cyberpunk, which featured a story line consisting of futuristic credit card fraud devices that were not yet manufactured, and characters who used them to steal and wreak havoc on the financial world of the future.

94

Chapter 10: The Best Policies, Procedures and Practices

Unfortunately, whomever the Secret Service was consulting about this case decided that Gurps Cyberpunk was actually a computer hacking manual, and they convinced the Secret Service that it had to be stopped immediately.

So the Secret Service swore out an affidavit and secured warrants for Steve Jackson Games and Loyd Blankenship's home and raided both, seizing both related and unrelated computer equipment and documents, which they refused to return for several years.

It took several years for the court case to wind its way through the system, but ultimately the Secret Service was harshly admonished by the presiding judge and SJ Games was awarded $50,000 and attorney's fees.

Normally this would not have been that big of a deal, but in reality, it showed just how far paranoia can infiltrate even a careful, studied, and literate group like the Agents of the Secret Service, because they acted without understanding the implications of what they were doing, or even the work they were performing, and without a clear understanding of the material they had alleged, in a legal affidavit, was illegal, when in fact that material was pure science fiction.

This case was the birthplace of the Electronic Frontier Foundation, a non-profit group of lawyers who provide legal services for those either wrongly or incorrectly accused of computer crimes, and that lobby for fair and legal laws relating to computer privacy and regulation. EFF is also very widely touted by computer privacy advocates who use it to argue that Government should have no authority to act in matters of computer regulation because they simply overreact and fail to fully investigate crimes "sometimes" and therefore should not be allowed to do it at all.

Whether you agree with this assertion or not, it should also be noted that fully 10% of all criminals lawfully executed in this country are determined to be innocent posthumously, so the healthy dose of fear by civilians against Government conspiracies and ineptitude isn't fully born of baseless fear. That number is based on the number of those found innocent by the Innocence Project and other groups and extrapolated to the general convicted population.[23]

Regardless, there are plenty of good solid reasons to be extra careful about how you determine you are accurately receiving intelligence about your specific target, and how to verify and double-check that. Every good Officer knows you corroborate and double-check everything, every chance you get, so that no innocent civilian has to suffer incarceration. That is basic Academy training and is borne out every day all across this great nation.

I tell you all of this to say this, there are plenty of criminals in need of your attention out there, and too many for us to catch them all, so let's just work together to keep each other and our constituents safe, and if we can bring someone safely to justice in the process, do it.

If you can't make your case the right way, don't make it at all, we all already know that.

This also brings up the problem of working with data in working servers and Data Centers. It's not uncommon for an employee of a business to have a rough day and start shooting people. That's a very unfortunate fact of life these days, and we all need to be prepared, because workplace shootings have become disturbingly commonplace.

When approaching a business with an embedded or barricaded suspect, you may find yourself dealing with multiple sources of network information, both wired, and wireless, and it may be very difficult to determine with any certainty exactly which stream of data your target is generating.

In fact, your target may not even be using the computer systems inside the business, particularly if they were terminated or no longer have access to the computer/network systems for other reasons.

In a situation like this, it is best to open as many scanning processes of both wired and wireless data as you can and try to get someone from the IT staff of the company to help you weed out the authorized data streams so that you can focus on those that may be generated by the target. With a

---

[23]http://www.innocenceproject.org/cases-false-imprisonment/front-page#c10=published&b_start=0&c4=Exonerated+by+DNA.

Introduction to Tactical Hacking: A Guide for Law Enforcement

multi-story building like an apartment complex or business center [think high-rise building New York City] you may find that you are not able to immediately isolate the traffic being generated by your target.

However, by carefully attenuating your signal detection strength and evacuating the surrounding apartments/business offices, you should be able to slowly wean out the signals not related to your target. After you complete the tactical mission, think about Steve Jackson Games before seizing computers, hardware, even paper documents. If you don't need them for a case against the Target, or if you can get the information in an acceptable copy format that will allow you to leave the original in place at the business, try to do that.

Our mission here is to ask the business to cooperate with us as we try to complete the task at hand. We don't need to seize everything and sort it out later. We can take the time to differentiate between needed data and documents critical to the business and not to our case.

In reality, in a data center with 50,000 or more industrial grade servers stacked in racks in a raised floor environment, you may not be able to find the exact hard disk containing the exact threatening message that you used to create the search warrant for entry and engagement, but if you photographed the screen when the message came in, you can argue "best available evidence" and that you didn't want to interrupt the daily business for a single message. You can actually do a forensic image of a working computer server, but I wouldn't recommend it without real solid skills and training behind you. You aren't likely to need it for a barricaded suspect or hostage taker anyway because their actions in barricading themselves and taking hostages will be sufficient for most criminal case charges against them anyway. The originating threatening message would be great to have, but it's unlikely to be necessary to include it unless it was all you had in the entire case against the person.

In short, do the right thing, for the right reason, and if he gets away today, someone will get him next time.

Be safe out there!!

Acknowledgements

I would like to dedicate this book to the most important people in my life, without whom I would never have taken the chance to try and put this material together:

My wife Becky, and daughter Katherine, who put up with long hours and helped me gather inspiration after long days and nights had sapped it thoroughly. My Father, Dr. Marc Neithercutt, who passed from this world on 12-16-2015 with my Mom and I at his side, on his own terms, leaving a void I doubt I'll ever feel inclined to even try to fill. I miss you Poppa. My Mother Janice, who has shown me the courage only a hero could muster after losing so many amazing people from her life in such a short period of time.

And my Aunt Janelle and her husband John Moncrief, two of the most gentle, loving, and supportive people I have ever met, whose presence is missed dearly by all of us in the family.

Introduction to Tactical Hacking: A Guide for Law Enforcement

Glossary

Most of this glossary was taken verbatim from the NIJ Special Report / Apr. 08, located at https://www.ncjrs.gov/pdffiles1/nij/219941.pdf

Analog: Also spelled analogue. A device or system that represents changing values as continuously variable physical quantities. A typical analog device is a clock on which the hands move continuously around the face. Such a clock is capable of indicating every possible time of day. In contrast, a digital clock is capable of representing only a finite number of times [every 10th of a second, for example].

Bandwidth: The amount of information or data that can be sent over a network connection in a given period of time. Bandwidth is usually stated in bits per second (bps), kilobits per second (kbps), or megabits per second (mps).

Bit-by-bit duplicate copy: The process of copying data stored on digital media so that it replicates the data at the lowest level. The term "bit copy" refers to the duplication of the zeros and ones (bits) that are the binary form of digital data.

BIOS: Basic Input Output System. The set of routines stored in read-only memory on a system circuit board that starts a computer, then transfers control to the operating system. The BIOS opens communication channels with computer components such as the hard disk drives, keyboard, monitor, printer, and communication ports.

Blackberry: A handheld device that functions as a cellular phone, personal organizer, wireless Internet browser, speakerphone, long-range digital walkie-talkie, and mini-laptop. Can be used to send and receive e-mail and text messages.

Blog: Derived from Weblog. A series of online journal entries posted to a single Web page in reverse-chronological order. Blogs generally represent the personality of the author or reflect the purpose of the Web site that hosts the blog.

BMP: A filename extension for Bitmap, an image file format generally used to store digital images or pictures.

Buffer: A block of memory that holds data temporarily and allows data to be read or written in larger chunks to improve a computer's performance. The buffer is used for temporary storage of data read from or waiting to be sent to a device such as a hard disk, CD-ROM, printer, or tape drive.

Cables: A collection of wires or optical fibers bound together, used as a conduit for components and devices to communicate or transfer data.

CAT-5/Category-5: A cable capable of transmitting data at high speeds (100 megabits per second and faster). CAT-5 cables are commonly used for voice and data applications in the home.

CAT-5e: Enhanced CAT-5. Similar to a CAT-5 cable, but with improved specifications.

CAT-6/Category-6 (ANSI/TIA/EIA-568-B.2-1): A cable standard for Gigabit Ethernet and other interconnect that is backward compatible with CAT-5, CAT-5e and Cat-3 cables. A Cat-6 cable features

98

more stringent specifications for crosstalk and system noise. The cable standard is suitable for 10BASE–T, 100BASE–TX, and 1000BASE–T (Gigabit Ethernet) connections.

CD/CD-ROM: Compact Disc—Read-Only Memory. A compact disc that contains data accessible by a computer.

CD-R: Compact Disc—Recordable. A disc to which data can be written but not changed or erased.

CD-RW: Compact Disc—Rewritable. A disc to which data can be written, rewritten, changed, and erased.

Chat Room: An Internet client that allows users to communicate in real time using typed text, symbols, or audio.

Compact Flash Card: A small, removable mass storage device that relies on flash memory technology—a storage technology that does not require a battery to retain data indefinitely. There are two types of compact flash cards: Type I cards are 3.3mm thick; Type II cards are 5.5mm thick.

Compressed File: A file that has been reduced in size by use of an algorithm that removes or combines redundant data for ease of transfer. A compressed file is generally unreadable to most programs until the file is uncompressed.

Cookies: Small text files on a computer that store information about what information a user accessed while browsing the Internet.

CPU: Central Processing Unit. The computer micro processing chip that contains several thousand to several million transistors that perform multiple functions simultaneously.

Deleted Files: Files no longer associated with a file allocation table or master file table. Deleted files are still resident on the media but are not accessible by the operating system.

DHCP: Dynamic Host Configuration Protocol. A set of rules used by communications devices such as computers, routers, or network adapters to allow the device to request and obtain an IP address from a server that has a list of addresses available for assignment.

Digital (photographs, video, audio): A digital system uses discrete values rather than the continuous spectrum values of analog. The word "digital" can refer to the type of data storage and transfer, the internal working of a device, or the type of display.

Digital Camera: A still camera that records images in digital format. Unlike traditional analog cameras that record infinitely variable intensities of light, digital cameras record discrete numbers for storage on a flash memory card or optical disk.

Digital Evidence: Information stored or transmitted in binary form that may be introduced and relied on in court.

DivX: A brand name of products created by DivX, Inc., including the DivX Codec, which has become popular due to its ability to compress lengthy video segments into small sizes while maintaining relatively high visual quality. It is one of several codecs, or digital data encoding and decoding programs, commonly associated with "ripping," where audio and video multimedia are

Introduction to Tactical Hacking: A Guide for Law Enforcement

transferred to a hard disk and transcoded. As a result, DivX has been a center of controversy because of its use in the replication and distribution of copyrighted DVDs.

Docking Station: A device that enables laptop and notebook computers to use peripheral devices and components normally associated with a desktop computer such as scanners, keyboards, monitors, and printers.

Documentation: Written notes, audio or videotapes, printed forms, sketches, or photographs that form a detailed record of a scene, the evidence recovered, and actions taken during the search of a scene.

Dongle: A copy protection or security device supplied with software. The dongle hinders unauthorized use or duplication of software because each copy of the program requires a dongle to function. Sometimes also used to describe a specialized USB device that is small or self-contained, like a Wi-Fi Dongle.

DSL: Digital Subscriber Line. A high-speed digital modem technology that allows high-speed data communication over existing telephone lines between end users and telephone companies.

DVD: Digital Versatile Disk. A high-capacity compact disk that can store up to 28 times the amount of data that a standard CD-ROM can hold. DVDs are available in DVD-R, DVD-RW, DVD+R, DVD+RW, and Blu-ray formats.

Electromagnetic Field: The field of force associated with electric charge in motion that has both electric and magnetic components and contains a definite amount of electromagnetic energy. Speakers and radio transmitters frequently found in the trunks of patrol cars are examples of devices that produce electromagnetic fields. So don't put anything digitally sensitive in the trunk of your patrol vehicle, or near any speaker of any kind.

Electronic Device: A device that operates on principles governing the behavior of electrons. Examples of electronic devices include computer systems, scanners, and printers. This is also known as any device that pisses off or confuses any of the older guys in the back of the room at briefing.

Electronic Evidence: Information or data of investigative value that is stored on or transmitted by an electronic device.

Electronic Storage Device: Any medium that can be used to record information electronically. Examples include hard disks, magnetic tapes, compact discs, videotapes, and audiotapes. Examples of removable storage devices include thumb drives, smart media, flash cards, floppy disks, and Zip® disks.

Encryption: Any procedure used in cryptography to convert plain text into cipher text to prevent anyone but the intended recipient with the corresponding key from reading that data.

EPROM: Erasable programmable read-only memory. A type of computer memory chip that retains its data when its power supply is switched off. Once programmed, an EPROM can be erased only by exposing it to strong ultraviolet light.

Ethernet: The standard local area network (LAN) access method that connects electronic devices to a network, cable modem, or DSL modem for Internet access.

Glossary

Exculpatory Evidence: Evidence that shows that a criminal charge is not substantiated by the evidence.

Faraday: A dimensionless unit of electric charge quantity, equal to approximately 6.02×10^{23} electric charge carriers. This is equivalent to one mole, also known as Avogadro's constant. Faraday isolation bags are used to prevent mobile phones and devices from connecting to communication signals.

File Format: Refers to file type based on file structure, layout, or how a particular file handles the information [sounds, words, images] contained within it. A file's format is usually indicated by the three- or four-letter file extension in the MS-DOS filename, e.g., .doc or .jpg.

Firewall: A firewall allows or blocks traffic into and out of a private network or a user's computer, and is the primary method for keeping a computer secure from intruders. Also used to separate a company's public Web server from its internal network and to keep internal network segments secure.

FireWire: A high-speed serial bus that allows for the connection of up to 63 devices. Widely used for downloading video from digital camcorders to the computer.

First Responder: The initial responding law enforcement officer or other public safety official to arrive at a scene.

GPS: Global Positioning System. A system of satellites and receiving devices used to compute positions on Earth. GPS is used in navigation and real estate assessment surveying.

GIF: Graphics Interchange Format. One of the two most common file formats for graphic images; the other is the jpg. Widely used on the Internet due to its high compression and subsequent small file size. GIF files have a .gif file extension and can be created or edited in most popular graphics applications.

Hard Copy: A permanent reproduction of data on any media suitable for direct use by a person, e.g., printed pages and facsimile [FAX] pages.

Hard Drive: A data storage device that consists of an external circuit board; external data and power connections; and internal glass, ceramic, or magnetically charged metal platters that store data. The most common types of hard drives are SSD and SATA, but also used to include IDE and SCSI.

Hardware: The physical components that make up a computer system such as the keyboard, monitor, and mouse.

Header: In many disciplines of computer science, a header is a unit of information that precedes a data object. In a network transmission, a header is part of the data packet and contains transparent information about the file or the transmission. In file management, a header is a region at the beginning of each file where bookkeeping information is kept. The file header may contain the date the file was created, the date it was last updated, and the file's size. The header can be accessed only by the operating system or by specialized programs.

Introduction to Tactical Hacking: A Guide for Law Enforcement

Hidden Data: Many computer systems include an option to protect information from the casual user by hiding it. A cursory examination of the system may not display hidden files, directories, or partitions to the untrained viewer. A forensic examination will document the presence of this type of information.

Host: A computer on a network that provides resources or services to other computers on the same network. One host machine may provide several services, such as SMTP [e-mail] and HTTP [Web]. Also the guy/gal who hands you a drink when you first arrive at the shift party.

IM: Instant Messenger. A type of communications service that enables users to communicate in real time over the Internet. Analogous to a telephone conversation but communication is text-based.

Internet Protocol (IP) Address: A 32-bit binary number that uniquely identifies a host connected to the Internet or to other Internet hosts for communication through the transfer of data packets. An IP address is expressed in "dotted quad" format consisting of decimal values of its four bytes separated with periods, e.g.,127.0.0.1.

IRC: Internet Relay Chat. A multiuser Internet chat client through which users communicate on channels referred to as chat rooms.

ISDN: Integrated Services Digital Network. A high-speed digital telephone line Internet connection.

ISP: Internet Service Provider. A business that provides access to the Internet. Small Internet service providers provide service via modem and ISDN, while larger ones also offer private line hookups like DSL and Cable.

JPG: Joint Photographic Experts Group. Also JPEG. A compression technique used for saving images and photographs. Reduces the file size of the images without reducing their quality; widely used on the World Wide Web.

Latent: Present, although not visible, but capable of becoming visible.

MAC Address: Also known as the hardware address. A unique identifier specific to the network card inside a computer. Allows the DHCP server to confirm that the computer is allowed to access the network. MAC addresses are written as XX–XX–XX–XX–XX–XX, where the Xs represent digits or letters from A to F.

Magnetic Media: Includes hard disk drives, tapes, cartridges, diskettes, or cassettes used to store data magnetically.

Media Storage Devices: Examples include disk drives, tape drives, Zip® drives, thumb drives, floppy disks, CDs, and DVDs. Unlike main memory, media storage devices retain data even when the computer is turned off.

Memory Card: A removable data storage device commonly used for storing images in digital cameras but can also be used to store any type of data. These devices are made up of nonvolatile flash memory chips in various forms such as CompactFlash, SD, Micro SD, SmartMedia, and Memory Stick.

Glossary

MiniDV: A videocassette designed for use in MiniDV digital camcorders. MiniDV cassettes can have up to 530 lines of video resolution.

MP3: An acronym for MPEG-1 or MPEG-2 audio layer 3. MP3 is the file extension for MPEG audio layer 3. Layer 3 is one of three coding schemes for the compression of audio signals. Layer 3 uses perceptual audio coding and psychoacoustic compression to remove the redundant and irrelevant parts of a sound signal.

MPEG: Moving Picture Experts Group. A standard for compressing full motion video. MPEG files frequently have an .mpg file extension.

Multimedia Player: A hard disk or flash memory-based electronic device, such as an MP3 player, capable of storing and playing files in one or more media formats including: MPEG, DivX, and Xvid, audio, MP3, WAV, Ogg Vorbis, BMP, JPEG, GIF, images, and interactive media Adobe Flash and Flash LITE.

Network: A configuration of independent computers, peripherals, and devices connected through data communication wires or wireless technologies capable of sharing information and resources.

Network Connection: A wired or wireless communication link between a group of computers or devices for the purpose of sharing information and resources.

Ogg Vorbis: An open-source audio encoding and streaming technology.

Operating System: A computer program that controls the components of a computer system and facilitates the operation of applications. Microsoft® Windows® Me, Microsoft® Windows® XP, Vista®, Windows 7, Windows 8, Windows 10, Linux, Android, and Apple® MacOS are common operating systems.

Original Electronic Evidence: Physical devices and the data contained by those items at the time of seizure.

Palm: Any of the various models of personal digital assistants marketed by Palm, Inc., a company that went out of business a long time ago, but had a pretty good product for a while. You still may find these around at a crime scene, and they may actually hold older file formats and data.

Password-Protected File: A file configured to deny access to users who do not enter the correct password (a specific character or combination of characters). Access denial security does not modify the content of the file; it only prevents those without the password from accessing it. Encrypted files, however, are actually scrambled into unrecognizable alphanumeric representations of the original data which can only be unscrambled by entering the correct password.

PCMCIA: Personal Computer Memory Card International Association. A trade association responsible for promulgating standards for integrated circuit cards, including PC cards and Express Cards.

PCMIA: Personal Computer Manufacturer Interface Adaptor. Used to expand the function of older personal computers.

Introduction to Tactical Hacking: A Guide for Law Enforcement

PDA: Personal Digital Assistant. A handheld device that can function as a cellular phone, fax sender, and personal organizer. Many PDAs incorporate handwriting and voice recognition features. Also referred to as a palmtop, handheld computer, or pocket computer, and currently represented as a "smart phone."

Peripheral: Any device used in a computer system that is not part of the essential computer, i.e., the memory and microprocessor. Peripheral devices can be external such as a mouse, keyboard, printer, monitor, external Zip® drive or scanner; or internal such as a CD-ROM drive, CD-R drive, or internal modem.

Personal Computer (PC): A computer whose price, size, and capabilities make it useful for individuals.

Phishing: Internet fraud perpetrated through an e-mail linking to a Web site simulating a legitimate financial organization; once on the fake Web site, victims are tricked into revealing a security access code, credit card or Social Security number, user ID, or password, which is then used by the thieves to
steal the victim's financial resources.

Phreaking: Old School Telephone system hacking. You know, back when phones had wires.

Printer Cable: A cable that connects a printer to a computer. You know, back when Printers had wires.

Port: An interface by which a computer communicates with another device or system. Personal computers have various types of ports. Internally, there are several ports for connecting disk drives, display screens, and keyboards. Externally, personal computers have ports for connecting modems, printers, mice, and other peripheral devices.

Port Replicator: A device that contains common computer ports (e.g., serial, parallel, and network ports) that plug into a notebook computer. A port replicator is similar to a docking station but docking stations normally provide capability for additional expansion boards.

Printer Spool File: The temporary file created when a print command is executed.

Processor: The logic circuitry that responds to and processes the basic instructions that drive a computer. The term processor has generally replaced the term central processing unit (CPU). The processor in a personal computer or that is embedded in small devices is often called a microprocessor.

PS2: PlayStation 2. A popular video game console.

PSP: PlayStation Portable. A handheld videogame console released in 2005 by Sony. Uses a Universal Media Disc and Memory Stick PRO Duo card for storage. The PSP also plays music and displays photos.

Quarantine: The status of any item or material isolated while pending a decision on its use.

RAM: Random Access Memory. Computer memory that stores data and can be accessed by the processor without accessing the preceding bytes, enabling random access to the data in memory.

Glossary

Remote: Files, devices, and other resources that are not connected directly to a computer.

Removable Media: Items that store data and can be easily removed from a computer system or device such as floppy disks, CDs, DVDs, cartridges, Thumb and USB Drives, and data backup tape and drives.

Screen Name: The name a user chooses to use when communicating with others online. A screen name can be a person's real name, a variation of the person's real name, or it can be a pseudonym (handle). Screen names are required for instant messaging (IM) applications.

Screen Saver: A utility program that prevents a monitor from being etched by an unchanging image. It also can provide access control. This was actually a critical function with the old CRT (Cathode Ray Tube) monitors because if your screen stayed open on a particular image for too long, it would "burn in" or create a shadow of the image you were looking at. This was a real problem with Security Camera Monitors.

Seizure Disk: A specially prepared floppy disk configured to boot a computer system and protect it from accidental or unintentional alteration of data. Now accomplished by use of a "write blocker" hardware or software device.

Serial Cable: Provided with a digital camera. Used to connect a digital camera to a personal computer so that images can be downloaded on to the computer hard disk.

Server: A computer that provides some service for other computers connected to it via a network.

SIM: Subscriber Identity Module. The SIM card is the smart card inserted into GSM cellular phones. The SIM identifies the user account to the network, handles authentication, and provides data storage for basic user data and network information. It may also contain some applications that run on a compatible phone.

Sleep Mode: Also Suspend Mode/Hibernate. A power conservation state that suspends power to the hard drive and monitor; results in a blank or powered off screen.

Smart Card: Also chip card, or integrated circuit card. A pocket-sized card with embedded integrated circuits which can process information. There are two broad categories of smart cards. Memory cards contain only nonvolatile memory storage components, and perhaps some specific security logic. Microprocessor cards contain volatile memory and microprocessor components.

Software: Computer programs designed to perform specific tasks, such as word processing, accounting, network management, Web site development, file management, or inventory management.

Stand-Alone Computer: A computer not connected to a network or other computer.

Steganography: The process of hiding files within other files.

System Administrator: A user who has the most comprehensive access privileges over a computer system.

Introduction to Tactical Hacking: A Guide for Law Enforcement

Temporary and Swap Files: To improve computer performance, many computer operating systems and applications temporarily store data from system memory or RAM in files on the hard drive. These files, which are generally hidden and inaccessible, may contain information useful to the investigator.

Thumbnail: A miniature representation of a page or an image used to identify a file by its contents. Clicking the thumbnail opens the file. Thumbnails are an option in file managers, such as Windows Explorer, and they are found in photo editing and graphics program to quickly browse multiple images in a folder.

Touch Screen: A video display screen that has a touch-sensitive transparent panel covering the screen. A user can touch the screen to activate computer functions instead of using a pointing device such as a mouse or light pen.

USB: Universal Serial Bus. A computer hardware interface connection that facilitates the use of many peripheral devices including keyboards, mice, joysticks, scanners, printers, external storage devices, mobile phones, smart phones, PDAs, and software dongles.

Virus: A software program capable of spreading and reproducing itself on connected computers and damaging or corrupting legitimate computer files or applications.

VoIP: Voice over Internet Protocol. The technology used to transmit voice conversations over a data network using the Internet protocol. Data network may be the Internet or a corporate Intranet.

Volatile Memory: Memory that loses its content when power is turned off or lost.

WAV: An abbreviation of Waveform. A type of audio file. Usually has a .wav file extension.

Wireless: Any computing device that can access a network without a wired connection.

Wireless Modem: A modem that accesses a wireless telephone system to provide a connection to a network.

Wireless Router: A network device that consists of a wireless access point (base station), a wired LAN switch, and a router to connect computers and peripheral devices to an Internet service. Wireless routers are a convenient way to connect a small number of wired and any number of wireless computers to the Internet.

Write Protection: Software or hardware that prevents data from being written to a storage device. Write protection ensures that digital evidence is not modified after it is seized.

Xvid: An open-source video codec library [video compression software] that follows the MPEG–4 standard.

Zip®: A removable 3.5-inch data storage disk drive. Sort of a predecessor to the CD-R and CD-RW.

Zip® File: A file that has been reduced in size to allow faster transfer between computers or to save storage space. Some compressed files have a .exe file extension, which indicates that the file is self-extracting.

About POLICE TECHNICAL

POLICE TECHNICAL is dedicated to providing the best in technical solutions and services to law enforcement and public safety.

Starting with one instructor teaching a single course (PowerPoint for Public Safety) POLICE TECHNICAL has steadily grown into a fully realized company complete with a management team and a score of instructors teaching at the highest levels of law enforcement throughout North America.

In 2014, POLICE TECHNICAL expanded its services beyond the classroom, shifting its position from being a technical training company to a solutions provider.

See **policetechnical.com** for a complete list of our training schedule.

Police Technical National Courses 2016

Applications for Public Safety™ -A total survey of law enforcement applications (apps), their effectiveness, and directions for personnel to create and deploy apps for their own agencies.

Cell Phone and Tablet Forensics™ - A cell phone forensic course for street level officer and supervisors. How the process works, what is possible (and what is not), how to handle digital evidence, what not to do, how to win in court.

Cell Phone Data and Mapping™ - Making sense of cell phone and tower data from cell phones. Providing visual representations of suspect and victim locations and criminal activity, timelines and Google map integration.

Cell Phone Investigations™ - Simply the most comprehensive course on cell phone examination and investigations. From the handset to the tower to the phone company to the courtroom.

Craigslist Investigations™ - Methods and tools for successful Craigslist investigations. Case examples include property related crimes, drug investigations, prostitution, and enticement of juveniles.

Emerging Technologies™ -Designed to help public safety executives prepare for technological changes in the public safety workplace. Case studies are presented to assist in the deployment and management of technology.

Excel® for Public Safety™ - Harnessing the power of Microsoft Excel® to better manage data and improve investigations. Telephone tolls, financials, arrest stats, fugitive lists and calls for service analyzed with a few clicks.

Google for Public Safety™ - Examines how public safety can leverage Google services for operations and investigations. More than just a Search also included are YouTube, Maps, Gmail, Google Voice, Drive and Apps.

Online Investigations™ - Designed to assist personnel become more proficient in online criminal investigations, an emphasis is placed on social media and proactive undercover investigations. Students will create UC online profiles, and deploy them using techniques learned in class.

PowerPoint® for Public Safety™ - Designed to assist all personnel become more efficient and proficient with PowerPoint® software, from basic design to case management; custom animation, video, audio, and Splash Screens®.

Social Media Methods™ - Designed to help departments and their personnel utilize social media effectively to manage their online presence; Designed to assist personnel in PIO, investigations and community relations position.

Tablets and Smartphones for Public Safety – Designed to assist agencies properly select, plan, deploy and utilize tablets and smartphones. Discussion includes various platforms and devices, best practices, and insight for current and future smart device purchases.

Word and Adobe for Public Safety - Designed to help personnel create, manage, share and protect public safety documentation. Emphasis is placed on creating agency specific branded themes, shareable templates, and custom reports.

In-Service Training

In-service training is the fastest, most cost effective way to provide technical training to personnel. POLICE TECHNICAL provides training for up to 40 people; an optional third day offers students additional hands-on time. Simplified pricing includes all expenses: Instructor fees, meals, travel, lodging, and training materials.

Contact the POLICE TECHNICAL office for rates and scheduling

812.232.4200 or info@policetechnical.com